"Children need a balance between screen time and other healthy activities." – American Academy of Pediatrics

BRILLIANT SCREEN-FREE STUFF TO DO WITH KIDS

A Handy Reference for Parents & Grandparents!

TEAM GOLFWELL

Brilliant Screen-Free Stuff To Do With Kids, A Handy Reference for Parents & Grandparents! Copyright © 2020, Team Golfwell. All rights reserved as to this work. No part of this publication may be reproduced, distributed, or transmitted in any form or by any means, including photocopying, recording, or other electronic or mechanical methods, without the prior written permission of the publisher.

Images in this book are from Creative Commons ShareAlike. All jokes, riddles, puzzles, one-liners, story jokes, etc. are fictitious.

There are references to other sites in this book and we do not control these sites and we neither are associated with nor have any business relationship with these sites.

Cover by Queen Graphics

DISCLAIMER

As parents and grandparents, you are most aware of what activities are safe for your individual child(ren) or grandchild(ren) since you know the nature and tendencies of the child. Please consider safety above all else before engaging in any activity suggested in this book.

The information contained in this book is for general information purposes only. We make no representations or warranties of any kind, express or implied, about the completeness, safety, accuracy, reliability, suitability or availability concerning anything in this book for any purpose. Any reliance you may place on such information is strictly at your own risk.

In this book there are links for the reader to look at websites or other material which are not under our control and the inclusion of these is for general information purposes only. We do not necessarily imply a recommendation or endorse the views expressed in those sites. You should always evaluate them yourself and/or seek proper and professional medical or emotional advice before engaging in any activity.

You understand any activity may entail known and unknown risks that could result in accidents, physical or emotional injury, or damage to property or third parties. Participation in an activity is purely voluntary and you elect to participate and assume all risks for yourself, and on behalf of your children, grandchildren, and your heirs, assigns, personal representative and your estate.

Neither the publisher nor the author is responsible for accidents, injury and/or damages incurred as a result of undertaking any activity referred to in this book. This book is not a substitute for medical or emotional professional services and before taking on any activity referred to in this book, competent advice should be first obtained from proper qualified medical or emotional practitioners.

FOREWORD

The American Academy of Pediatrics (which is probably today's best authority on what's good for kids) has gone on record saying children need a balance between screen time and other healthy activities.[1]

This book is a one-stop reference packed with off-screen activities for kids and ideal for parents and grandparents for gobs of healthy stuff for them to do. With over 350+ screen-free activities, this book will provide you with very entertaining substitutes for digital games, tablets, laptops, TV, etc.

Parents, Grandparents, and most importantly kids should enjoy this book to get active, socialize, have lots of fun, and enjoy a healthy balanced life!

The activities (and their page numbers) are grouped under Chapter headings for quick reference. The Chapters are alphabetically arranged in the extensive "**DIRECTORY**."

Brilliant Screen-Free Stuff to do With Kids

The purpose of this reference book is to quickly suggest ideas for activities when you need to keep kids active and get them quickly interested, prevent boredom, and get their minds off annoying issues, irritability, and/or sedentary screen activities.

Although most activities are completely described, for conciseness we refer to sites online for very detailed or additional information on some of the activities since this book would be too voluminous if we were to detail and give additional information on all of them. There are a few important educational on-screen activities (NASA, NOAA, Climate Change sites, etc.) that are strictly for learning and having a lot of fun while learning.

We hope you, your children and grandchildren use this reference book often and enjoy the variety of activities in this book and create many happy life-long memories together!

The DIRECTORY of Activities begins on the next page.

DIRECTORY

FOREWORD 1

DIRECTORY 3

AVIATION FOR KIDS 35

    Free introductory flights for kids with "The Young Eagles." 35

    EAA online aviation course for kids grades 2 - 5. 35

    Learn to Fly EAA Programs for kids 36

    Redbird Landing 36

    FBO – Fixed Based Operators 36

    Major Airports 37

    Hot air ballooning 38

    Hot Air Ballooning for Children with Special Needs 38

BEACH FUN 39

    Scavenger hunt at the beach 39

- Conchology. 43
- Royal Sandcastles 44
- Protect the castle (future engineers will like this) 44
- Beach soccer 45
- Boogie Board 45
- Sand hopscotch 45
- Sand tic-tac-toe 45
- Limbo lower now! 45
- Frisbee Toss 46
- Fill the bucket relay 46
- Kite flying 47
- Volleyball 47
- Beach Tug of War 48
- 4-way Tug of War 48
- Beach Ball Blanket Toss 48

Blowing Bubbles on the beach.............. 49

Make Sand Angels 49

Make a sand person(s) and decorate 49

Sand Art & Sculpting Family Figurines... 50

Trace figures in the sand 50

Create a keepsake hand sand print....... 50

Collecting smooth rocks 51

Shoreline "Ring Around the Rosie."....... 51

Squirt gun beachball race 52

Decorative jar of sand......................... 52

Cookie-cutter sand shapes 53

Musical beach towels 53

Snorkel and mask 53

Beach bowling 53

Wave Tumble Rocker game 53

Armless beach ball races 54

Sand Darts 54

Alphabet learning in the sand 54

Make a Beach Sundial 55

Beach shoe toss 55

Silly beach photo fun 55

Beach tent... 55

Beach inflatable pool........................... 56

Guess what I'm drawing...................... 56

BEDTIME – TROUBLE SLEEPING? 57

Sing a Lullaby 57

Quiet talk about the day...................... 58

Writing in a journal before bed............. 58

Keep the lights on for 10 minutes so they can wind down 58

Darkness and temperature 59

No soda after 2 pm............................. 59

Focus on relaxed breathing 59

Focus on a soothing word 60

Reading a book 60

Avoid noise 60

Turn off the screens 60

No heavy exercise. 61

Weekends – Try not to stay up later 61

Leaving the rest enjoying the night 61

How much sleep do they need? 62

More Ways to get them to sleep 62

Recite Goodnight Poems 64

Write to Jimmy Fallon 64

BRAINSTORMING GAMES – LATERAL THINKING 65

Expand Your Brain Game. 65

Rhyming 66

Expanding Vocabulary Games 67

Ingenious salesperson game 68

Word chaining (from the Japanese game of Shiritori). 69

Brainteasers - Kids Environment and Kids Health 70

BUCKET LIST – Summer Activities 71

Sample Summer Vacation Bucket List ... 71

Educational Bucket List 77

CALISTHENICS AND STRETCHING 78

Fitness exercising. 78

Martial Arts 78

Join in sports with them 79

Motivating your kids to exercise 79

Losing weight and exercising just for kids 79

CALMING ACTIVITIES - To Ease off Tantrums 80

Deep breathing 80

Jumping rope 80

Hot baths 81

Cold showers for elevating moods 81

Fish watching 81

Count backward from 100, or try coloring books and drawings 81

Deep belly breathing 82

Listen to them 82

Hugging for 20 seconds 82

Take turns doing the "Copy Cat Game .. 82

15-minute walk 83

Writing it out 83

Writing out appreciation gives a positive attitude 84

Crinkling tissue paper 84

Popping bubble wrap 84

Roll a golf ball under the foot 85

Playing music 85

Letting it all out! 85

Riding Bikes, Running, 50 Jumping Jacks, etc 85

Tell a Personal Funny Story 86

Ride a bike. 86

CLIMATE CHANGE – ENVIRONMENTAL AWARENESS GAMES 87

Climate change for kids 87

Kids make their own rainbow! 87

NASA'S site about the Earth 87

EPA Ozone Crossword Puzzle 88

Learn about air quality. 88

Build your own air quality sensor 88

Energy Kids 88

Healthy animal environments............... 89

Recycling games for small children 89

Creatively pass the recyclables 89

Plastic bottle bowling 90

Tin or aluminum can-stacking 91

Newspaper (no dropsy) relay 92

Smokey says. 93

Yellowstone Park 93

Kids Environment and Kids Health 94

CONVERSATION GAMES TO GET THEM TALKING 95

Guess how we met 95

When I was your age game 95

Make Three Wishes............................. 96

Best Dishes (meals)............................ 96

Worst Food 96

Best and worst thing of the day 96

Appreciation 96

Favorite Movie 97

Foretell the Future.............................. 97

Favorite Vacation Place 97

Loving Parents 97

Growing Self Esteem 97

Developing Interests........................... 98

Fact or Fiction 98

Positive Character Trait Game.............. 98

Bowl of Questions............................... 99

DANCING GAMES 102

Create a dance move........................102

Musical Dancing Chairs. 102

Crazy ball dance................................103

Crazy Animal Dance for young kids......103

Balloon juggle dancing. 104

Crazy Jumping Energy Expender Dance 105

Impromptu Emotion Dancing 105

DISABILITIES OR SPECIAL NEEDS ACTIVITIES 107

Animals, Zoos, Animal Trainers. 107

Animal Shelters................................107

Fire Stations 108

Hot Air Ballooning 108

Police Stations 108

Trainspotting 108

Aviation 108

Greenhouses 109

Botanic Gardens...............................109

Kid Calisthenics................................110

Slamming a medicine ball....................110

Exercise videos 110

Build confidence...............................111

Blind children..................................111

AD/HD Activities - Perform a script......112

AD/HD Legos 112

Kids with AD/HD - Teach them photography......................................112

Kids with AD/HD - sports....................113

Asperger Syndrome - Drama classes ...113

Kids with Asperger and libraries and Legos...113

Sites with events especially for kids with special needs....................................114

EDUCATIONAL SCREEN STUFF – BRIGHT AND INTRIGUING 115

CODESPARK Academy........................115

Khan Academy Kids 116

PBS KIDS 116

Starfall... 116

EVENING FUN ACTIVITIES................ 117

For Grandparents - Skype Grandparents and vice-versa! 117

Hand and Foot Massages.................... 117

Set a time for going to bed................. 117

Evening swim 118

Invite adult friends to evening dinner ..118

Appreciation time for you 118

Camping out in the family room 118

Reading aloud and acting out stories ...119

Jigsaw puzzles 119

Coloring books and reading books 119

Act out the "Kids Theatre 119

Star Gazing 120

Catching fireflies 121

Evening night walk 121

Board games 122

Establish an evening routine 122

Evening hugs before bedtime..............122

INDOOR OR RAINY DAY FUN 123

Kids Theatre 123

Take a trip to the local museum or aquarium 124

Bowling with gutter guards.................124

Indoor skating rinks...........................124

Indoor pools 124

Family movies....................................125

Local movie theatres..........................125

Family board games 125

Make a hideaway indoor fort 125

Find the treat 125

Dancing 126

Magic shadows 126

Playing cards 126

Ask kids to write a children's book 126

Baking 126

Make a paper airplane 127

Reading aloud with your kids will help them succeed. 127

Read stories from children's picture books to kids 3-5 128

Reading aloud to any child 128

Read a screenplay together aloud 128

Read books 128

Legos 129

Make puppets 129

Grannie's Jewelry Box. 129

Dress up. 130

Child Meditation 130

JOKE TELLING TIME...........................131

Telling Riddles and Jokes.....................131

Riddles..132

Sample Jokes and Riddles 132

LIBRARY ADVENTURES 143

Look for the biggest book 143

Research recipes in cookbooks............143

Rainy day reading 143

Audiobook section. 143

Find the "How to draw" books section ..144

Children's book clubs 144

Teach them how to check out books, and eBooks, etc. 144

Newspaper & Magazine Section 145

Future Writers 145

Travel Section 145

Future Chefs and more cookbooks 145

Quotations, Poetry 146

Have fun in the reference section 146

Computers 146

MAGIC TRICKS FOR LITTLE WIZARDS 147

Magic freezing water 147

Magic pre-sliced banana in its own peel 147

Find the chosen card 148

Magic pepper repel 149

Magically guess anyone's age 149

Read minds! Magically guess any number! 150

The magical number 37! 152

Many other magic tricks 152

MEMORIES – PRESERVING THEM 153

Digital Scrapbooking 153

Instagram or other Photo Printing 153

Establish a tradition to strengthen bonds 154

Tell them about yourself, Grandparents 155

Help the world and talk about it 155

For Grandparents. A reminder and ways to make grandchildren feel special and needed 156

Record your story with them and store it on StoryCorps.org 156

MINUTE TO WIN IT GAMES 157

LOL Minute to Win It Games 157

OUTDOOR ADVENTURES – WONDERS OF NATURE 158

Avoiding "Nature Deficit Disorder 158

Feeling tree bark 158

Summer berry picking 159

Wildflower picking 159

Tree growth rings..............................159

Feed wild birds with breadcrumbs........160

Winter bird feeding 160

Start a campfire with a magnifying glass
....161

Pitch a tent or make a shelter 163

Nature Photography and General.........163

Hiking and Exploring..........................165

Survival 165

Orientating 166

A Lesson on Poison Ivy 167

Bike Trails and Mountain Biking...........167

PHOTOGRAPHY 168

Time-lapse photography 168

Color or Alphabet Photography for small children 168

Show them the basics of good photography 168

    Fill the frame 168

    Pointing or leading lines 169

    Cropping 169

    Rule of thirds 169

    Window light 169

Start with an inexpensive camera 170

Teach them to take candid photos 170

    Learn more 170

PIE IN THE FACE FUN 171

Whipped Cream Pie Spelling Bee 171

Whipped cream math quiz 173

Find the jellybean in the pie 173

Apple bobs with no hands....................174

Finish the bowl..................................174

PIZZAS AND OTHER STUFF 175

Developing future chefs 175

How to make the basic pizza...............175

Strange and Unusual Pizzas................176

Funny face pizzas 177

Other stuff. 177

Mom's or Grandma's Pita sandwich...177

Mom's or Grandma's Macaroons.......177

Teach Family recipes 178

Dishes for age groups. 178

RAINING? THERE'S STILL A LOT OF FUN OUTSIDE!.. 179

Worm hunting...................................179

Jumping puddles and singing 179

Make boats out of recyclables 180

Make a paper boat............................180

Make a cardboard boat 180

Homemade boat races 180

Blow bubbles in the rain....................181

Follow the rain 181

Measuring rainfall............................181

RIDDLES – BRAIN BUSTER RIDDLES FOR VERY SMART KIDS........................... 182

SAFETY SLOGANS TO SHARE............ 188

Teach safe procedures 189

Dial 911..189

Strangers......................................189

Fires – Home fire drills....................189

Stop Drop and Roll 190

Electrical Outlets 190

Hot stovetops 190

Microwaves 190

Safety slogan quiz 191

Crime prevention and safety tips. 193

Playground safety 193

SCIENCE FUN 194

Making Magic Crystals 194

Ivory soap - make a puffy cloud soap bar
.... 195

Carnations coloring themselves 196

Fizzy Oranges 197

Rainstorm in a glass 197

More Easy Science Experiments for Kids
.... 198

SNOW – FUN IN THE SNOW 199

Sledding & Tobagganing 199

Snow Sculptures 199

Big Snowball Roll..................................199

Creating snow people 200

Snowpeople fashion show...................201

Pin the nose on the snowman 201

Snowball toss 201

Snowball target practice....................202

Tic Tac Toe in the snow......................202

Shovel snow for the unfortunate 202

Start a snow shoveling business..........202

Make hot chocolate with snow............203

Snowball fights and snow fortresses 203

Snow amusement parks.....................204

Snow towns.......................................204

Identify and photograph animal tracks in the snow 205

Follow the very cool (but silly) leader...205

Tug of War in the Snow......................205

Build a snow picnic table 205

Snow soccer 206

Snow Dodgeball 206

Snowball toss and pyramid cup tower ..206

STORYTELLING FUN......................... 207

Begin by you telling a story about how you met your husband or wife...................207

Tell a story about when you were a child 207

Tell a story about when the child was born 208

Grandparents can tell a story about their early experiences with their grandchild. 208

Grandparents, tell them a story your grandparents or parents told you 208

Tell a story about your first day at your first job 209

Tell a story about how you solved an issue 209

Tell a story about how you solved a nagging problem 209

Tell a story about what you liked as a kid 209

Ask your children or grandchildren to tell you a story 210

Tell a story on how you got in trouble at school 210

Tell a story that made you proud 210

SWIMMING POOL FUN 211

Create Your Own Synchronized Swimming, Swim Dance or Water Ballet 211

Solo Swimmer – Things to Do 211

Play music 212

Underwater camera 212

Beach ball or water polo ball race 212

Ping Pong ball pool race 213

Keep fit with Pool Volleyball 213

Towel on head tag game 213

TEACH SOMETHING MEMORABLE 214

Teach them a skill 214

Ride a bike 214

Teach them to swim 214

Teach them to cook 215

Ancestry 215

TEEN ACTIVITIES 216

Aviation and Aerobatic Flying 216

Bridging the gap with questions 217

Show your teen grandchild a photo of yourself as a teen................................219

Be positive. 219

Grandparents, tell stories on how you transitioned to an adult......................220

Go to a sporting event together 220

Fishing, Hiking, Gardening, Cooking, Exploring trips 220

Minute to Win It Games 221

Ask for help with your computer..........221

Attend their events............................222

Show unconditional love....................222

Ask about their friends......................222

Fine dining 223

Figure Skating, Bowling, Tennis, Soccer, etc. 223

Parent – teen disputes 223

Bonding with a teen grandchild – sharing mutual interests...............................224

Ask your teen to interview you and store on StoryCorps.org 224

Cook together at a family event 224

Take a class together..........................225

Sharing Grandma's Jewelry with Teens 225

Read the same book 225

TODDLER AND THREE TO FIVE-YEAR-OLD ACTIVITIES 226

Toddler presents in a bathroom bowl. ..226

Toddler tub party 226

Spider web a doorway with sticky tape.226

Simon says...227

Number treasure hunt.........................227

Water glass xylophone 227

Cardboard box fort. 228

Dress up 228

Make popsicles...................................228

Sidewalk chalk activities......................228

Chalk draw mom and dad 229

Draw a bullseye target for bean bag toss 229

Alphabet square word hop 229

Trace letters 229

Jigsaw Puzzles 229

Warmer and Colder 230

Scavenger hunt 230

Hide and Seek 230

Toddler Dance Party 230

TONGUE TWISTERS 231

Toddlers verbalizing 231

Help the toddler talk 231

Toddler sing-along 231

Tongue Twisters 231

VEGETABLE GARDEN FUN 234

ANSWERS TO BRAIN BUSTER RIDDLES 237

About the Authors **245**

"A computer once beat me at Chess. But it was no match for me at Kick Boxing!"

-Emo Phillps

"Families should proactively think about their children's media use and talk with children about it, because too much media use can mean that children don't have enough time during the day to play, study, talk, or sleep," - *Jenny Radesky, MD, FAAP Lead author of the policy statement of the American Academy of Pediatrics*

AVIATION FOR KIDS

Free introductory flights for kids with "The Young Eagles." A flight in a small plane like a Cessna 172 is an unforgettable experience for kids that will be remembered all their lives. Since 1992, The Young Eagles organization has given over 2 million first free rides to kids ages 8 – 12. The Young Eagles organization wants to introduce aviation to kids and was founded by the EAA. EAA volunteers offer free flights to kids. Here is their website for further information for flying opportunities near you>

https://www.eaa.org/eaa/youth/free-ye-flights

EAA online aviation course for kids grades 2 - 5. The EAA also has an 81-page study course for kids who want to learn more about aviation, weather, etc. on this site >

https://www.eaa.org/en/eaa/eaa-chapters/eaa-chapter-resources/~/media/6238df775d7b4398819edc3247463ab5.ashx

Learn to Fly EAA Programs for kids. See this site to learn about more opportunities to learn how to fly with The Young Eagles too > http://www.aviation-for-kids.com/learn-to-fly.html

Redbird Landing. The Redbird Landing organization constantly releases new information about the aviation world. They are a group of flight instructors, flight school managers and general aviation enthusiasts who are interested in teaching young people about aviation. They offer many free opportunities to introduce kids to aviation. https://landing.redbirdflight.com/posts/introducing-youth-to-aviation-is-an-investment-in-the-future

FBO – Fixed Based Operators. If there is a small airport near you, stop in to see the manager and learn about free introductory flight opportunities for kids. FBOs are in business managing aircraft, fueling, repairs, renting planes, and general aviation. Flying clubs are usually based at small airports and the manager or the bulletin board most likely has more information on introductory flying opportunities through flying clubs, etc. You may also find Learn to Fly Programs specifically for kids.

Ask permission to take your kids or grandkids out on the tarmac to view the planes tied down. You may see the small planes take off and land and get a close look at the tied down planes. Touch the wings, propellers, see the controls, gauges, instruments, put a headset on them to listen to the control tower, etc. During slow times you may even get a chance to go up and visit the control tower if you ask about for permission from the airport manager.

Major Airports. At major airports, watch the planes take off and land, see the shuttles, moving walkways, escalators, baggage handlers, etc. Some major airports have observation parks specifically designed to watch takeoffs and landings like the Raleigh Durham International Airport >

https://www.rdu.com/general-aviation-a-great-place-to-view-planes/

Hot air ballooning. Hot air ballooning may be difficult for kids since they may not be tall enough to see over the edge of the basket. Ask the balloonist if kids are allowed before you venture out to get a ride.

This site has a list of hot air balloon organizations that may give you more information on hot air ballooning opportunities for kids.

http://www.usairnet.com/hot-air-balloon/organizations/

Hot Air Ballooning for Children with Special Needs. This site has a list of organizations that offer hot air ballooning experiences for children with special needs. It would be an amazing ride for the child who will remember you arranged it for them and be remembered by them all their lives. See >

http://www.blastvalve.com/Balloon_Rides/Special_Needs/

BEACH FUN

The hardest part of going to the beach may be trying to convince the kids it's time to go home! But if they need things to do, this Chapter is very helpful for things to do at the beach.

Scavenger hunt at the beach. Scavenger hunts will keep them busy. Here is a list of objects (delete or add items as you like) for your children or grandchildren to search for on the beach. Offer a small prize (an ice cream, chocolate bar, toy, etc.) to the one who finds the most in a half-hour or one hour or whatever time you decide.

To avoid children picking up the wrong things, and if your kids or grandkids have phones, ask them to take pictures or videos of these instead of picking them up and putting them into a bucket.

You can also divide your kids or grandkids and any others who want to join into teams and offer a prize to the winning team.

You can make up your own list according to the beach or lake you're going to. And, you can make the list longer by asking for larger numbers of the items than in the sample list below (e.g., find 7 different colored beach rocks instead of 4, or 3 snails instead of one, etc.).

- 4 different colored beach rocks
- A small piece of kelp or seaweed
- A small piece of driftwood
- A snail
- Photos of bird tracks, dog tracks, etc.
- A photo of a crab walking in a shell
- A photo of a certain kind of boat
- A photo of a wet animal
- A photo of a sport (e.g. volleyball) being played at the beach
- A photo of a surfer in action
- Photo of someone in a one-colored green (or choose any color) bathing suit, one-piece or two-piece suit, etc.

- A photo of the largest footprint in the sand
- Ditto for the smallest footprint in the sand
- A photo of a fisherman
- A photo/video of feeding the seagulls, a seagull landing for a cracker, and the seagulls flying off.
- A photo of the team buried up to their knees in sand or a video of the whole process.
- A photo of a specific number such as 4 (or more) seagulls (or birds) in a single photo.
- A photo of a completed sandcastle as high as their bucket (or two or three buckets tall, etc.) with turrets on top and flagpole.
- A video of them singing whatever beach song (or any song) they choose like, "By

the Beautiful Sea," or "Surfin' USA", etc. You can ask them to dance while singing it too.

- If they are old enough and it is safe enough (i.e., there is a lifeguard present) ask them to get all wet and come out of the water (or a shower) and roll in the sand and become a "scary and creepy sand person" from the neck down avoiding any sand on their head or hair. Take a photo too!
- A video of them telling a made-up story (at least 30 seconds long, or another segment of time) about the "one that got away" reenacting the fishing struggle and concluding by holding up their hands showing how big the fish was.

- A photo of a street sign starting with the letter "C" (or whatever letter(s) you choose).
- A photo of a good-looking man and or woman
- A photo of them or the team (less the picture taker) in midair jumping safely into the water or safely off a small curb onto the sand.
- Photo of them or the team climbing on a jungle gym.
- A close photo of a flower
- A close photo of an insect
- A sneaky candid photo or movie of you.

Please make up your own list of items and ask for photos or videos of anything interesting and safe.

Conchology. The children may develop a lifelong interest in shells. Rare shells such as the Wentletrap shell and others can be worth thousands of dollars. In any event, finding pretty seashells that can be used for later art projects lead into yet another activity of doing shell art projects which are simply creating art with shells.

Let them use their imagination on how to arrange the shells and what materials they want to use to create the artwork. There are numerous things to create with no limits. For more info on creating shell artwork see > https://www.wikihow.com/Category:Shell-Art-and-Craft

Royal Sandcastles. Build a grand sandcastle and decorate with figurines, kings, queens, princesses, dragons, dragons, knights, flags, etc.

Protect the castle (future engineers will like this). Tell them about the changes in the tides and the changing shoreline. Build a castle near the water's edge and as the tide comes in, ask them to build a castle and figure out how to prevent their castle being washed away using rock barriers, moats, canals or whatever they come up with.

Beach soccer. If the beach is not crowded, a fast game of beach soccer will make them sleep a lot better in the evening.

Boogie Board. Boogie or bodyboards are great exciting fun, exercise, and amusement riding waves. If you are not familiar see this > https://www.wikihow.com/Boogie-Board

Sand hopscotch. Draw a hopscotch diagram in the sand and use seashells as markers.

Sand tic-tac-toe. Draw a tic-tac-toe diagram in the sand and keep score in the sand.

Limbo lower now! Limbo is a lot of fun at the beach and others around you may join in the limbo fun. Even more fun if you have music playing too.

If you have music, anyone waiting their turn in line must be dancing to the music. Bring a bamboo pole or a simple dowel or a jump rope, etc. and set it up.

Most know how to play limbo - two people hold the pole. Contestants line up to see who can get under the pole without touching it and knocking it down while keeping their balance. If they can't get under the pole, knock the pole down, or touch the ground with anything except their feet, they are eliminated. The rest of the kids (and any adults who have joined in) line up again after lowering the pole a bit. This site has 3 variations of the limbo game >https://www.wikihow.com/Limbo

Frisbee Toss. Set up a target a distance away such as a seashell, bucket, hole in the sand, or another marker. The children take turns behind a line in the sand to see who can toss the frisbee the closest to the target. Keep score in the sand and play to 11 or 21. Of course, the younger the children, the closer the target. Older kids can set up a very distant target or even several targets.

If you happen to be on a large uncrowded beach, the children could design their own "Frisbee Beach 3 hole (or even 9 or 18 holes) Golf Course" and see who can complete the course with the least number of tosses!

Fill the bucket relay. Each team has the same size bucket and they must rush to the water, fill their water carrying objects such as a paper cup (or other water carrying tools such as a spoon for older kids) and fill a bucket. They all start at the same start line, run to the beach and fill up the cup or spoon, etc., then run back to their bucket trying not to spill any of the water and put the water in the bucket. The team that fills their bucket first wins! Lots of excitement and fun! Pick new teams and repeat. You can also play this game, one child against another.

Kite flying. If the beach isn't crowded most children love the thrill of flying a kite. There are all kinds of kites. Sport kites, box kites, huge kites, small kites, etc. Delta Kites (triangular-shaped) are usually the easiest to fly and are very popular. You need a moderate amount of wind for successful flying. Have a contest to see who can fly the highest kite. Wear sunscreen and eye protection and avoid looking into the sun.

Volleyball. Depending on the ages of the kids playing, volleyball on the beach is great fun so if you know there's a volleyball net at the beach bring a volleyball.

For the very young children use a beach ball and a towel stretched out as a net or on the sand. Count the number of times the very young ones can get the ball back and forth or have them keep score. Challenge them to get the ball back and forth 5 times or more!

Beach Tug of War. Bring a long rope and have the teams line up against each other along the water's edge. Draw a line in the sand and have the middle of the rope lined up with a line in the sand or an object. Start the Tug of War by shouting "Pull!" You act as the judge to see which team can pull the rope to their side. Yes, they will most likely all end up in the water. Lots of even more fun if there are big waves! See which team wins 2 out of 3 or whatever you decide. Pick new teams too.

4-way Tug of War. If there are lots of kids involved, there is a variation called "4-way Tug of War" with each team pulling 4 ends of two ropes tied in the middle and extending out in 4 directions. Feel free to join in as well!

Beach Ball Blanket Toss. Use a large beach towel or blanket and children each hold a corner or end depending on how many are playing. Put a beach ball in the middle of the towel and toss it into the air to see how high up they can toss the ball in the air. Ask them to count how many times they consecutively toss it up and catch it in the blanket! Challenge them to toss it 7 times or more!

Blowing Bubbles on the beach. The beach is usually a very safe place to blow bubbles in all shapes and sizes. The kids will chase them. See who can make the largest bubble. See who can make the smallest bubble. See who can make the most bubbles in one blow. Or just play it for fun!

Make Sand Angels. It's fun and messy. It is the same as making snow angels in the snow. Yes, they will have sand in their hair so you may not want to do this. Take pictures!

Make a sand person(s) and decorate. Just like making snowmen and snowwomen. Start small and use wet sand. Decorate the sand persons with shells, sticks, seaweed hair or beards, shell necklaces, feather moustaches, etc. to make it more creative. Take a close-up photo too. If it works with small sand persons, try making a larger one(s).

Sand Art & Sculpting Family Figurines. Use wet sand and their imagination to create sand families or whatever sand sculpture meets their fancy. They can spend hours on this especially if you bring a bucket, shovel, water spray bottles with food colorings, etc. to help them create their masterpiece. Take photos. Here is how to do this in detail > https://www.youtube.com/watch?v=-USzKmQ4Ahw.

Trace figures in the sand. A child lays down in the sand and the other kids trace the figure. Take turns so all have traces of themselves in the sand. Then ask them to decorate the figures with sunglasses, shells for eyes, sticks for the nose, seaweed for hair, beard and eyebrows, and use paper plates, paper cups, or whatever to create a masterpiece.

Create a keepsake hand sand print. Kids love to see how small their hands were as the years go by. Craftingagreenworld.com offers free, simple, easy and detailed instructions on how to make a keepsake handprint or footprint in the sand using plaster of Paris > https://craftingagreenworld.com/articles/beach-craft-make-a-sandy-handprint-keepsake/

Collecting smooth rocks. Find smooth rocks that the kids or grandkids can use later for painting for a remembrance of the day you brought them to the beach. A few smooth rocks are ideal for crafts to do indoors on a rainy day. Acrylic paints are best on rocks after they are washed and cleaned. See this very detailed YouTube (there are others too) for basic instructions on how to best paint rocks for beginners or use your imagination > https://www.youtube.com/watch?v=VN0pmfPn4VI&list=RDCMUCpLHSHJVlhI8NOYdWBluoYg&start_radio=1&t=23

Shoreline "Ring Around the Rosie." Play this very simple and age-old game at the shoreline or in shallow water at the shore's edge. You will hear the lots of laughs when it comes time to the "All fall down" part at the end! This is also a great game to get used to the water temperature!

Squirt gun beachball race. Two children or teams of children can compete against each other to see who can push a beach ball from the start line to the finish line using squirt guns (you can use spray bottles too).

A variation of this game is to draw two lines opposite each other ten feet apart (more or less) with a beach ball in the middle. Each team kneels behind their own line and on the word "go" each team (walking on their knees) uses squirt guns or spray bottles to try and push the ball over the other team's line to score a point. Play the game to whatever points you decide.

Decorative jar of sand. The children can make their own decorative jars by filling a jar with different colored sand, pebbles, seashells, etc. Mark the date on the jar as a reminder of when it was created. Here is a site on how to make very beautiful sand jars > https://www.youtube.com/watch?v=9dhPgsp4kIQ

Cookie-cutter sand shapes. Use cookie cutters to make interesting sand displays. Use paper cups, buckets, etc. too.

Musical beach towels. This is played the same way as musical chairs only use beach towels instead of chairs. Lots of fun!

Snorkel and mask. Always interesting especially if you teach them how to snorkel for the first time. Earplugs and/or nose plugs are very good to use too. Ask them to search the sandy bottom for shells and interesting things.

Beach bowling. Fill plastic bottles, or cans, with water or sand and bowl them over with a volleyball, or soccer ball. Keep score to see who wins. Play as many frames as you wish.

Wave Tumble Rocker game. On a day when waves are breaking and washing ashore, have the kids sit on the shoreline holding their arms around their knees waiting for each wave as it breaks to shore. The force of the waves should make them roll backward. When the wave recedes, they should try to roll forward to their original position. The trick to this game is to see who can keep holding their arms around their knees the longest without letting go when the big waves wash ashore!

Armless beach ball races. If you have several children, divide them up into teams of two. Have a start and finish line. The teams compete to see which team can carry a beach ball from the start line to the finish line without using their arms.

Sand Darts. Draw a dartboard in the sand with point values in each ring. The grandkids toss small stones or shells instead of darts to score. Play to 100 or whatever score you choose.

Alphabet learning in the sand. Learn the ABCs at the beach. Draw letters in the sand and teach the letters to the small kids as you draw them and make the sound the letter represents. Try drawing words too and teach them to read simple words.

Make a Beach Sundial. Teach the children how to tell time without a watch. Most of us know how to make a sundial and here is a simple article giving a lot of detail on how to do this.
https://www.education.com/activity/article/Make_Sundial/

Beach shoe toss. Throughout Florida and other southern states, kids and adults compete to see who can toss a mullet fish (or another fish) the farthest. Instead of a fish, use a beach shoe, flip flop, beach ball, etc. to see who can toss it the farthest.

Silly beach photo fun. Ask the children to come up with a silly, goofy, or any kind of original posing for a photo of themselves individually or in a group. The sillier or the more creative the better. Keep it and show it to them in later years.

Beach tent. Kids love to make tents. Use palm or tree branches, umbrellas, beach chairs and towels and have them make up their own beach shelter.

Beach inflatable pool. Toddlers enjoy their own inflatable pool at the beach. Bring an inflatable pool to pump up for them. Ask the other children to carry sea or lake water to fill it up. Take pictures to show family teamwork.

Guess what I'm drawing. On slips of paper, write down the names of different objects or animals (starfish, crab, a giraffe, cow, lifeguard stand, etc.) and put them in a bucket. The kids take turns each selecting a slip of paper then drawing the object in the sand. The other kids must guess what is being drawn and the first to guess gets a point. Take turns drawing and the one who guesses 7 correctly wins (or any number you chose).

> "Having kids is like living in a foreign commune. Everything is sticky and you're not sure why." - Anon

BEDTIME – TROUBLE SLEEPING?

Science Daily reports recent research has shown, "One big problem with school-age children is it can take them a long time to get to sleep, so avoiding activities like playing video games or watching exciting movies before bedtime was important..." [2]

These are ways to put children to sleep and to start a habit of establishing a good routine to get the right amount of healthy sleep each night. Sleep is magical and necessary to allow their entire body to rejuvenate and be ready for the next day.

"Good sleep hygiene gives children the best chances of getting adequate, healthy sleep every day... Research tells us that kids who don't get enough sleep on a consistent basis are more likely to have problems at school and develop more slowly than their peers who are getting enough sleep." [3]

Sing a Lullaby. "Hush Little Baby Don't You Cry", "Twinkle-Twinkle Little Star", "You Are My Sunshine" and others are great lullabies. Here is a site with the lyrics to these old songs

>https://www.sleep.org/articles/best-lullabies-for-kids/

You may have favorite songs you like to sing. Spotify also has numerous lullabies on it such as "Somewhere Over the Rainbow", "Danny Boy", and many more.

Quiet talk about the day. Talk about the day and let the child express how they feel and what they enjoyed the best. Answer their questions and keep it toned down.

Writing in a journal before bed. If you give your child or grandchild a journal to write down their thoughts and writing about what they want to do tomorrow. Writing things down will help get thoughts out of their minds so they can have a clear mind and fall asleep easier. This works well for adults too. [4]

Keep the lights on for 10 minutes so they can wind down. Turning out the lights right away may prevent relaxation. Tell them the lights (perhaps soften the lights too) will be on for 10 minutes (or whatever you wish) to give them a chance to say a prayer, make a journal entry, etc.

Darkness and temperature. The darker it is the more conducive going to sleep becomes. Also, a cooler (but not cold) room is generally better than trying to sleep in a hot room. The right pajamas should be chosen since temperatures tend to drop at night. If your child or grandchild is not used to sleeping overnight in a new place and is afraid of the dark, a dim night lite generally helps, of course.

No soda after 2 pm. Many soft drinks contain sugar and/or caffeine which will keep the child awake as you know. A warm glass of milk or a few crackers might be the right thing if they are hungry at bedtime.

Focus on relaxed breathing. Ask your child to watch their body as they inhale and exhale slowly. Ask them to notice how their body moves while they breathe. Their stomachs should slowly rise and fall if they breathe slowly and properly. Suggest they start at 100 and count backward from 100 by slowly inhaling and exhaling. Tell them to casually notice how relaxed they feel while doing it.

Focus on a soothing word. Tell your child to think of a soothing word like "peace" or "flower" or "calm" etc. Ask your child to slowly think the word to themselves before each breath, then take in a slow breath and exhale slowly and repeat the word slowly before taking the next slow breath, and so on. Tell them to not let their mind wander off. Calmly suggest they dismiss any interfering thoughts before thinking of the peaceful word before each breath.

Reading a book. For older children, reading books generally will help them go to sleep as it gets their minds off themselves and any issues.

Avoid noise. Generally, quiet is conducive to help the child go to sleep. Sometimes, the child may find the total quiet deafening. If so, try a fan or something which makes a peaceful rhythmic sound to help the child go to sleep.

Turn off the screens. Watching screens such as TV, computer games, etc. tells the brain to stay awake and decipher the information. Turn these off or even keep them out of the bedroom to avoid temptation. [5]

No heavy exercise. Exercise gets their heart pumping making it difficult to calm down when it's time to go to bed. Heavy exercising should not be done 3 hours before bedtime. Hopefully, they will have had enough exercise during the day since regular exercise in the daytime helps them calm down easier in the evening.

Weekends – Try not to stay up later. Staying awake longer during the weekend will disrupt their internal clock. It may even be starting a bad routine of staying up late on weekends when they're not ready for that yet. It is generally recommended not to disturb their internal clock and their established "going to sleep routine." [6]

Leaving the rest enjoying the night. Keep in mind, a child needs to blend into downtime. It is difficult for a young child to go to bed when the child sees others staying up enjoying themselves. You might try to put them to bed when others in the house are reading or doing things the child has no interest in.

The time for going to bed should be non-negotiable. As kids grow, most of us know sleep comes easier if there is a routine with a definite bedtime, and a usual wake up time all of which helps set their biological clock.

Have a calm environment, a cool temperature, and a large focus on relaxation. But if that doesn't work, try these ways to help them go to sleep fast.

How much sleep do they need? First, you need to know, of course, how much sleep they need depending on their age. Toddlers 1-3 year-olds usually need 12-14 hours of sleep, 3-6 year-olds need 11-12 hours, and 7-12 year-olds need 9-10 hours.

More Ways to get them to sleep. Children generally take 15 to 30 minutes to fall asleep once they get into bed. If they absolutely cannot sleep, perhaps you might check with their pediatrician to make sure your child doesn't have a sleep disorder. If there are no disorders, see what your pediatrician advises.

You might try these suggestions to see if they work.

1. The age-old warm glass of milk and crackers.

2. A very warm bath for 15 minutes before bed with soft music playing.

3. Make sure all electronics are removed and none can be heard like TV background noise.

4. Suggest they read their favorite book or give them their favorite book(s) to view the illustrations themselves. Check on them and turn the light off when they're done.

5. Encourage them to talk about what's keeping them from sleep.

6. Read a simple story to them softly.

7. Talk gently with them about why they can't sleep to have them verbalize it. Don't try to solve it, just listen and let them talk it all out of themselves.

8. Do they have their stuffed animal for security?

9. Try to ignore repeated requests like one more drink of water, etc. Don't give in. Let them know once they're in bed it's time to let their body refresh with healthy sleep.

10. Establish rules that TV, video games, etc. are not allowed within one-hour of bedtime. [7]

11. The Mayo Clinic has an excellent article on getting preschoolers to sleep. Check it out > https://www.mayoclinic.org/healthy-lifestyle/childrens-health/in-depth/child-sleep/art-20044338

Recite Goodnight Poems. Reading poems to them like, "Wee Willie Winkie", "The Sugar Plum Tree", "In a Garden", and many more well-known poems will help relax children> http://poemsforkids.org/5-goodnight-poems-for-your-sleepy-kids/

Write to Jimmy Fallon. Ask your child to write a letter to Jimmy Fallon at The Tonight Show. There is a special email for kids' letters. The email is > kidletters@tonightshow.com.

BRAINSTORMING GAMES – LATERAL THINKING

Expand Your Brain Game. Sit down with your children or grandchildren and show them several ordinary objects such as a fork, spoon, hairbrush, etc. Put the objects on display in front of you. Give the kids several minutes to come up with different uses for each of them.

For example, a fork can be used to pick up food from your plate. But if you would happen to sharpen one side of the fork you could use the sharpened side of the fork as a cutting utensil or a knife to cut food on your plate into smaller more edible pieces. You can also use a fork to mix food, stir a liquid, poke open a clogged small opening, etc.

Show them more ordinary items and give them several minutes to think about it, then ask them for their ideas. The more original the better!

You can also make this more fun when you ask them to come up with different uses for their toys.

If they have trouble with this game, ask them to give you an object and you come up with different ideas for them so they can watch how you do it.

Rhyming. You could inspire your children and grandchildren to become future poets. Start by asking them how many words they can come up with to rhyme with a word such as "rain" or "fan." Here are others.

Simple words like, Toy, Jane, bird, bone, bun, cent, frame, far, win, fit, (make up your own too).

Medium words to rhyme like, starter, word, puzzle, bark, cyst, etc.

Very difficult words to rhyme like, harder, harbor, sparkler, purple, etc.

FYI: If you are ever stumped on finding a rhyming word see this site that has a massive rhyming generator that poets or songwriters use in writing rhyming songs or poetry > https://www.poemofquotes.com/tools/rhyme-generator/

Expanding Vocabulary Games. Sit with your children or grandchildren and play music. Give one of them something they can pass to each other such as a toy (or a microphone, or a ball - whatever is handy) and tell them you are going to give them a question or a topic and the one holding the toy has to come up with a word or phrase about that subject.

For example, the question or topic you can start with could be words that begin with "S", or,

- Names of different cars
- Names of different pets
- Names of different languages
- Names of different sports
- Different types of music, etc.

After you give the first child a topic, see what answers the child comes up with. After the child is through, the child passes the object to the next child and the next child must likewise come up with a word or phrase about that subject and the process continues until you stop the music. When the music stops, the one holding the object must talk for 30 seconds about that subject.

Then start again with another topic or subject.

You may be surprised at how much they know.

Ingenious salesperson game. You start this game by trying to sell your children or grandchildren something they don't want or need. For example, try to sell them a broken umbrella, or a broken shoelace, or last year's wall calendar, or a dead battery, or a shoe or a sock with a hole in it, etc.

After you show them how to sell it ask them to try to sell things they don't want or need to you. Your children or grandchildren may surprise you to show how creative and persuasive they can be.

If they can't come up with crazy things to sell, a list follows with items to sell and feel free to come up with your own – the funnier the better! They could try to sell you,

- Left-handed baseball glove
- A flyswatter with a hole in it
- A paper cup with a hole in the bottom
- A sock with a hole in the toe
- A jump rope with a broken rope
- A staircase that goes nowhere
- Diet water
- A tennis racquet with no strings
- A rubber ball that doesn't bounce,
- A Bulgarian dictionary, etc.

Word chaining (from the Japanese game of Shiritori). You say a word such as "toy" and the next person has to come up with a word beginning with the last letter of the word "toy". For example, this is a sample chain where the next word begins with the last letter of the word announced,

To_y_ – _y_ar_d_ – _d_ir_t_ – _t_im_e_ – _e_ar... and so on.

If the next person incorrectly says a word or can't come up with a word that begins with the last letter of the last word said, he or she is eliminated, and the play continues until there is one person left. This game improves both spelling and vocabulary.

Brainteasers - Kids Environment and Kids Health. This is on-screen stuff but very educational. The National Institute on Environmental Health has a site specially designed for kids that teaches them about the environment and a lot of aspects of our ecology and how important it is. This site has entertaining Brainteasers, Puzzles, Riddles, Songs, and much more things to learn about our environment and it's very entertaining> https://kids.niehs.nih.gov/games/index.htm

It also has games, coloring, activities, and learning lessons already for you and it's very interesting and beneficial for them especially on rainy days or indoor play days. > https://kids.niehs.nih.gov/activities/index.htm

BUCKET LIST – Summer Activities

Kids grow up fast as we all know and there are things many people feel every kid should do while still a kid as shown in the Sample Bucket List that follows.

A bucket list will also motivate them to get themselves off-screen and outdoors. Completing the list will improve their confidence and self-esteem. The following is only a sample and make your own children's bucket list according to their age, likes, and dislikes.

Sample Summer Vacation Bucket List

___Catch a fish at least 1 foot long

___Hike through the forest with a compass

___Stargaze and find a constellation like the Big Dipper, Orion's Belt, the planet Venus, etc.

___Build a sandcastle with a moat

___Fly a kite to at least a 100-foot altitude

___Pack a picnic basket and picnic on a beach

___Make a work of art by melting crayons with a hairdryer on a wood carving. See this > https://www.youtube.com/watch?v=KFGpi5yoz8U

___Make a work of art with colored chalk on a sidewalk and take a photo of it

___Create and perform a puppet show with sock puppets or paper bag puppets

___Design a paper boat and win a paper boat race.

___Feed seagulls on a beach and see how many gather.

___Write a children's story with your own words and illustrations.

___Catch 25 fireflies in the evening

___Dance ballet in a rain shower

___Gather 25 Seashells

___Plant a tree

___Plant a vegetable garden

___Go Kayaking

___Make up and bury a Time Capsule and mark the spot it's buried with a painted stone

___See a shark, sawfish, and an octopus in an aquarium

___Go to the museum and find something you did not know ever existed

___Slide down the longest or steepest water slide in a waterpark near you

___Ride the fastest roller coaster in your area.

___Find the reference book section in the Library

___Visit a farm and bring back cheese, fresh fruit and vegetables, or something unusual

___Visit Dad at Work

___Visit Mom at Work

___Visit Grandma at Work

___Visit Grandpa at Work

___Ride Your Bike on a long bike trip to a relative's or friend's house. Plan your trip yourself and map it out. Get it approved by your parents before doing it.

___Shoot a score under 40 at miniature golf.

___Do a kind act

___Get three strikes in a row bowling

___Ride the largest Ferris wheel in your town

___Have a water balloon fight

___Swim one-half or one mile non-stop using freestyle, breaststroke, sidestroke, and backstroke

___Wash the family cars

___Learn how to make homemade ice cream

___Roast Marshmallows on a safe campfire you started without matches

___Have a root beer float

___Eat ice cream for breakfast

___Eat what you eat for dinner for breakfast

___Help Cook Dinner

___Make Fresh Lemonade and share it

___Read at least 3 books

___Research and make up your own Science Project

___Play Dodgeball with water balloons

___Organize a Family Game Night

___Organize a Slumber Party with a pillow fight

___Write what you accomplish in a Personal Journal describing what you did this Summer and how you felt about each activity

___Have a dance party

___Make an obstacle course on the beach

___Do yoga exercises for 15 minutes

___Teach your dog a new trick

___Write a poem

___Write a children's story

___Make your own lunch

___Bake your favorite cookies by yourself

___Write a letter to both grandparents

The bucket list activities will give the child plenty of things to tell their teacher and class when asked, "What did you do during summer vacation?"

Educational Bucket List. The bucket list can be educational with things like,

___Learn a musical instrument

___Learn how to greet and thank people in 7 different foreign languages

___Learn a second (or third) language

___Take an art class

___Learn how to draw a cartoon figure

___Create your own comic strip

Add anything you want to this list to help them learn what they like to do.

CALISTHENICS AND STRETCHING

Fitness exercising. Kids spending too much time indoors sitting around might find themselves overweight or not fit.

Fitnessblender.com has a 25-minute exercise video just for kids. They throw in games with their special kid's exercise video like "Red Light Green Light" and "Jump or Drop" and more and it's a lot of fun for kids! See > https://www.fitnessblender.com/videos/fitness-blender-kids-workout-25-minute-fun-workout-for-kids-at-home

You might even want to do the 25-minute exercise video with your kids or grandkids and its great fun! Here is the Fitness Blender link to the video > https://youtu.be/McD6_oOWs-M?t=5

Martial Arts. Learning martial arts builds confidence and self-esteem. If your child or grandchild is being bullied or if you sense they lack a bit of confidence, they may have an interest in learning defensive Martial Arts. Check out local Martial Arts learning centers in your area.

Join in sports with them. Kids love it when you join in and play sports with them such as simply throwing a baseball or a football back and forth. Or, try taking a hike together through the woods or local park (e.g., taking the dog too for a long walk together), or ride bikes together, etc.

Motivating your kids to exercise. This site has a very comprehensive article on how to motivate and persuade your children to exercise and have an interest in fitness > https://www.wikihow.com/Motivate-Kids-to-Exercise

Losing weight and exercising just for kids. This is a very comprehensive article showing you how children can not only lose weight but also get fit in healthy ways > https://www.wikihow.com/Lose-Weight-and-Exercise-More-While-Still-Being-a-Kid

CALMING ACTIVITIES - To Ease off Tantrums

Kids are known to throw tantrums. So, what do you do when you see a tantrum coming on?

Deep breathing. Deep breathing gets more oxygen to the brain. If your child refuses to deep breathe, light a candle and ask your child to blow it out. Doing so will make the child take a deep breath. Once they blow out the candle, move the candle six inches farther away and relight the candle and have the child blow it out again, and so on. If you don't have a candle, try blowing a pinwheel, or blow up balloons. Discontinue if they feel faint or have any issue with deep breathing.

Jumping rope. Jumping rope for 2 minutes gives a calming effect. Add music too. Challenge your child or grandchild to see if she can jump rope (or play hopscotch instead) for 2 minutes straight.

Hot baths. A hot bath will calm and soothe stressed-out kids. The warm water relaxes the muscles and relieves tension.

Cold showers for elevating moods. On the other side of the coin, a cold shower has been known to elevate moods from feeling sluggish and annoyed to feeling invigorated. Cold showers reduce tension, fatigue, and negative moods. Challenge them on a very hot day to see if they can sing one of their favorite songs in its entirety while taking a cold shower.

Fish watching. Watching fish swim reduces a person's blood pressure and has a relaxing effect. A visit to an aquarium or a trip to a lake or simply watching a goldfish swim in a bowl is calming, especially with soft music playing.

Count backward from 100, or try coloring books and drawings. Focusing on numbers will get your child's or grandchild's mind off what's bothering them. Or sing 99 bottles of beer on the wall. It will simplify their thoughts. Coloring books or drawing pictures will also make them focus on something else than what is bothering them.

Deep belly breathing. Tell your child or grandchild the belly is like a balloon. Ask them to take a slow deep breath raising their bellies, and then slowly exhale.

Listen to them. Verbalizing their problems helps. Encourage them to talk about what is bothering them. Don't try to solve their problem, just let them vent and let them talk it out and they will gradually feel better the more they talk about it with all their feelings being verbalized.

Hugging for 20 seconds. A 20-second hug has been shown to elevate feelings of wellbeing, reduce blood pressure, and relieve stress.

Take turns doing the "Copy Cat Game." This is a very simple game to get the kids out of bad moods or tantrums. Parent(s) or grandparent(s) and the kids all sit in a circle in the center of the room. The game is started by the first person who has the earliest birthday in the year doing a silly antic - whatever they wish to do such as making a silly face, pat their head and simultaneously rub their stomach, do a silly walk, do a silly dance, etc. The funnier the better!

Then starting from that person's left, the next person copies whatever the first person did. Then the next person to the left does the same antic, and so on until everyone takes a turn copying it the first silly antic.

Then have the next person to the left do a silly antic, and so on. The game continues for 2 or 3 go arounds or however long you wish.

Any child in a bad mood learns to focus on what the others are doing and gets his or her mind off what's bothering them.

15-minute walk. A simple walk of 15 minutes or more in the park, around the block, etc. has been shown to reduce stress and elevate a person's mood. [8]

Writing it out. For older children, writing out what is bothering them may calm them down and give them a chance to slow down and think about their feelings. Tell them no one will read it. If they know it's private, writing it out to themselves might elevate their mood.

Give them a sheet of paper, or a journal, or notebook and remind them you will not read it (unless they give it to you to read). [9]

Writing out appreciation gives a positive attitude. Ask your child or grandchild to write out in a journal or on a piece of paper things they are thankful for which is a "Thank You Journal." Instead of mulling over an issue, the child writes about things they are very thankful for. Encourage them to write in their "Thank You Journal" whenever they feel depressed or annoyed.

Crinkling tissue paper. Babies like the sound and feel of crinkling tissue paper. The sound and feel of this somehow cause them to focus on the newness of the sound and touching it gives them the feel of a new texture. "Peek a boo" is another way to get them to focus. Or, picking them up and showing them paintings or pictures high up on the walls gives them something brand new to focus on.

Popping bubble wrap. Very popular if there is any bubble wrap around. This diverts their attention and has them focus on something other than what's bothering them.

Roll a golf ball under the foot. The bottom of the foot has pressure points to relieve stress. Rolling a golf ball under the sole of the child's foot will trigger these points causing relaxation.

Playing music. Music is well known to elevate moods and divert attention. Try different types of music.

Letting it all out! So long as it won't disturb neighbors, ask them to let out a primal scream. One way to do this is to have them stand up and focus on all their bad feelings and frustrations and let those bad feelings and frustrations boil up and rise in their bodies and blast out of their mouths!

Riding Bikes, Running, 50 Jumping Jacks, etc. If the child is throwing a tantrum, consider exercising. Exercise will relax a child since it produces endorphins which reduce stress in the brain. Exercise with them if you are able. Check out this Harvard Health Publishing Article about exercising to relax >

https://www.health.harvard.edu/staying-healthy/exercising-to-relax

Tell a Personal Funny Story. You might tell a story about something unusual that you went through when you were their age. For example, tell a story about what you dressed up as for Halloween, or a crazy birthday party you went to, or seeing circus performers do a crazy performance, etc. Then ask the child to tell a funny story about themselves.

Ride a bike. Balancing on a bike, viewing outside scenery and getting stimulus from things around them as they ride may help calm down as well.

**"Having a 2-year-old is like having a blender, but you don't have a top for it."
– Jerry Seinfeld**

CLIMATE CHANGE – ENVIRONMENTAL AWARENESS GAMES

Climate change for kids. Climate change is important to all of us and especially our kids. This chapter lists activities that are educational on-screen activities. Climate change is a very real thing as we all know. [10]

Kids make their own rainbow! NOAA features weather games for kids and has a site just for kids to begin to learn about weather. See the games on NOAA's "SCI JINKS" site that gives kids excellent ways to learn about how weather works along with a general understanding of weather. It teaches them about Hurricanes, Rain, Rainbows and even how to create their own rainbow, and more > https://scijinks.gov/menu/games/

NASA'S site about the Earth. NASA has a site called "Climate Kids" which is just for kids to learn about climate change > https://climatekids.nasa.gov/

Kids can also learn why the sky is blue, how much water is on the Earth, how far away the moon is, and much more about the Earth. > https://spaceplace.nasa.gov/menu/earth/

EPA Ozone Crossword Puzzle. The Environmental Protection Agency has a crossword puzzle for kid's grades 4-7 to learn about ozone. https://www.epa.gov/ozone-layer-protection/ozone-science-crossword-puzzle

Learn about air quality. Air quality changes daily. Kids can become more aware of the daily air quality and learn how to see if it's good or not good by checking this site > https://airnow.gov/index.cfm?action=airnow.main

Build your own air quality sensor. Older kids can learn how to make their own air quality sensor from household materials > https://www.epa.gov/climate-research/build-your-own-particle-sensor

Energy Kids. Here is a site where kids will learn a lot about energy and have fun doing it! The US Energy Information Service has a site full of games, funny riddles, and science experiments. It teaches them about energy > https://www.eia.gov/kids/games-and-activities/riddles/

Healthy animal environments. The Smithsonian Science Education Center has games for kids teaching them about animal environments and their needs. Kids love animals and should find it very interesting > https://ssec.si.edu/habitats

Recycling games for small children. Plastic bottles sit in landfills or float in oceans for thousands of years. The sections that follow in this chapter feature fun games involving plastics and other recyclables to learn the importance of recycling.

Creatively pass the recyclables. This game needs several to play and it's a great game when there are lots of kids around. Ask the kids to pick teams so they are divided into two or more groups. Ask the two teams to line up and at the front of each team's line, put a pile of recyclable materials on the ground and place recycling bins at the end of each team's line.

On the word, "Go" the kids must pass the recyclables from the beginning of the line to the end of the line where the last person in line deposits it in the correct recycling bin. The catch here is the members of each team must pass the item in a different way than how they received it. The first team finished wins.

For example, when one team member passes the recycling item to the next, that person passes it on in a different way than the way he or she received it. For example, if the first team member handed the recyclable item, then the next team member must think up and use a different way to pass it such as, through their legs, behind their back, over the shoulder, etc.

Plastic bottle bowling. Fill up 10 (more or less) plastic bottles partially with sand so they easily stand up. Pace off 10 steps on your lawn (or whatever you feel is appropriate) from the foul line and place the plastic bowling pins upright in the form of a triangle like bowling pins. The kids take turns bowling using an appropriate ball. Use bowling rules and 10 frames (or whatever number you like). Recruit a pin spotter to re-stand the pins after each frame.

Unless you want to reuse the bottles for another game, have the kids collect, empty and dispose of the plastic bottles (as well as any other plastic materials in your area they can find) into a recycling bin or drop them off at the recycling center.

Tin or aluminum can-stacking. Tin and aluminum cans are easily recycled and preserve our natural resources. Give each child or grandchild a bag of cans and ask them to build the highest stack of cans they can without tipping over. Make sure the shapes and sizes of the cans are roughly the same or try it with different shapes and sizes to see how creative they can be. They can bend or shape them and use their imagination and know-how on how to stack their cans in their bag as high as possible. Whoever has the highest stack wins. Or, you can play this game with a goal of whoever uses the most cans in their structure that doesn't collapse wins.

Then mix up the cans and have another game with each child having different cans. Play 2 out of three, or 3 out of five games to see who wins. Take a movie of it to show their engineering and construction abilities. Ask them to look for any other cans in the area and return the cans to the recycling bin or recycling center.

Newspaper (no dropsy) relay. Recycling newspapers saves trees. Also, paper thrown away in the landfill creates methane gas as it breaks down. Give each child a big stack of newspapers and help them take the stack behind the start line. On the word, "Go" each child takes as many newspapers as they can and carries them 50 yards (or whatever distance you choose) and puts them in a paper recycling bin.

Then they run back and get more newspapers until they have carried all the newspapers from the starting line to the bin. If they drop any paper on the way to the bin, they must stop, pick up the dropped newspaper and bring it back to the starting line and re-try to carry a pile to the bin without dropping any. The first one who has all his newspapers in the recycling bin wins.

After the game is finished, ask them all to look around the area for more paper as well as any recyclable materials and pick them up and bring them back for recycling or to the recycling center.

This game can also be done with teams.

Smokey says. "Only you can stop forest fires." The fires in Australia were devasting in 2020. Safe campfires are extremely important. This is a site is for kids to learn about how to build safe fires and techniques to prevent them. It has activities and games just for kids to learn these techniques> https://smokeybear.com/en/smokey-for-kids

Yellowstone Park. If you are planning a trip to the Yellowstone Park in the US, this US Park Service site is just for kids to learn all about this US National Park including its geysers, interesting wildlife and much more >

https://www.nps.gov/yell/learn/kidsyouth/index.htm

Kids Environment and Kids Health. The National Institute on Environmental Health has a site teaching kids the importance of our environment with puzzles, riddles, songs, etc. It also has games, coloring, and lessons ready for you and might be something very interesting to do especially on rainy days. > https://kids.niehs.nih.gov/games/index.htm

There are no passengers on spaceship earth. We are all crew. - Marshall McLuhan

CONVERSATION GAMES TO GET THEM TALKING

There are times when it's difficult to get a teen talking and these games might be useful to get the conversation flowing. Also, useful if you want to change the subject of the conversation at the dinner table. Try some of these conversation games to produce very interesting conversations.

Guess how we met. The children or grandchildren take turns telling how they think dad and mom met (if they don't know already) or how grandma and grandpa met. After they are finished guessing, you reveal the true answer and tell a story about it.

When I was your age game. This is a game where you tell the children or grandchildren about something you did or something that happened when you were the same age as the children or grandchildren. Tell a story for each child's age. Then the kids must say what they think they will be like when they are parents and when they are grandparents.

Make Three Wishes. This is an old game, but it seems to usually get them talking. Ask them what they would wish for if a magical genie gave them three wishes.

Best Dishes (meals). What is the favorite dish that mom makes and what is the favorite dish dad makes? Likewise, what's the favorite dish grandma and grandpa make?

If they can cook, or want to cook, ask them to describe their favorite dish and how they would prepare it.

Worst Food. Ask them what the worst food was they ever ate. Then you tell them the worst food you ever ate. For example, did you ever have peanut butter on a hot dog?

Best and worst thing of the day. Take turns and go around the table and everyone tells what the best thing and the worst thing was that happened to them that day.

Appreciation. Everyone around the table says what they are most thankful for this past week. At Thanksgiving, everyone around the table says what they are most thankful for since the last Thanksgiving.

Favorite Movie. Everyone around the table tells what their favorite movie was and why it is their favorite.

Foretell the Future. Everyone around the table tells what they think they will be like in 5 or 10 or 20 years from now.

Favorite Vacation Place. Everyone around the table tells their favorite vacation spot and why it is their favorite.

Loving Parents. The children take turns explaining what mom, dad, grandma, and grandpa do to make them feel the most loved. You explain what your folks did to you to make you feel the most loved.

Growing Self Esteem. The parents or grandparents begin by explaining what they most like about themselves, i. e., what is their best quality? Then the children say what they like most about themselves.

Developing Interests. Everyone around the table describes what they like to do the most and why? What do they want to be when they grow up? And, how they plan right now to accomplish it?

Fact or Fiction. Everyone around the table takes a turn and tells three things about themselves. Two of the things must be true and one of them must not be true. The others take turns guessing which one is not true. Keep score and see who guesses correctly the most. Play to 3 or 7, or any number you like.

Positive Character Trait Game. Write these traits (and any other positive traits you like) on little slips of paper and put the little slips of paper in a bowl. One of the parents or grandparents begins and picks a trait out of the bowl, reads it aloud, then names another person or persons at the table who he or she feels has that trait and explains the reasons why. The bowl is passed to the left and the next person picks a slip of paper with a trait on it and does the same until all the traits are discussed.

Here are a few positive traits to write down on small slips of paper, Smart, Honest, Loyal, Respectful, Kind, Humble, Courageous, Calm, Cheerful, Understanding, Patient, Considerate, Confident, Devoted, Relaxed, Open-Minded, Energetic, Happy. (add as many more positive traits as you wish).

Bowl of Questions. Occasionally, you pick up your child or grandchild from school or an event and the child who has been interacting and talking with other kids all day tells you nothing about what went on at school or the event. If you don't want to keep asking, it may be more helpful to play this game at dinner to get them talking.

Write these simple questions out on slips of paper and put the slips in a bowl. As you sit around the table, pass the bowl around and each person picks a question from the bowl and reads it aloud then answers it. The following are only sample questions and please delete any you don't like and add any questions you do like.

If you were the principal at school what would you change about it?

If you were to hide a treasure chest and bury it what would you put in the treasure chest and why?

What is the best gift you ever gave anyone?

What was the best gift you ever received?

What was the craziest thing that happened in school this week?

What was the funniest thing that happened in school this week?

What have you done this week that you made you feel very good?

What frightens you the most?

What is your favorite time of each day?

What is your favorite food for breakfast?

What is the best thing an adult can do that a child can't do (and vice-versa)?

What do you most love about yourself?

What celebrity would you like to meet and why? What would you ask the celebrity?

If you could change anything in your life, what would you change?

Who is your best friend and why?

Who is the worst person you know and why?

What is your favorite and worst subject at school and why?

Do you believe in aliens, and if so, do you think aliens are living here on Earth secretly?

If you could change anything about your life, what would you change?

What are the best ways to make a friend?

(So not to be too obvious, mix questions about the topic you want to know more about from your child with fun and intriguing questions.)

DANCING GAMES

In any of the dancing games that follow, feel free to join in and dance with your children or grandchildren!

Create a dance move. This game enhances creativity and memory. Have one child stand in the middle and tell the child when the music starts, he or she must make up a short dance move (they can give a name to the dance move too).

The next child steps into the center and repeats that dance move and adds an additional short dance move to the previous dance move. The next one repeats the original dance move and the second dance move, and then adds a new short third dance move, and so on.

Any dancer who can't repeat the correct succession of dance moves is out and the next dancer continues until only one dancer remains.

Musical Dancing Chairs. This is played the same way as musical chairs except the chairs are placed around and outside of the dancing area. When the music stops the children must <u>dance</u> their way to the chairs. If they run instead of dancing, they're automatically out.

Crazy ball dance. This game is just for laughs and there are no winners or losers. One of the children holds a small ball that won't break anything (e.g., a whiffle ball, a softball, etc.) and when the music starts the child holding the ball begins to dance. The child at any time can toss the ball to another child and once that child catches the ball or picks it up, he or she must begin dancing. The dancer then dances until he or she tosses it to another player and so on. The dancing continues until the song is over. The child holding the ball restarts dancing when you begin the next song and so on.

You can play this game for fun, or you can play it by eliminating the person who last tossed the ball when the music stops and see who can last the longest.

Crazy Animal Dance for young kids. To start the game, you call out the name of an animal, then all the children make the sound of the animal. Then they use their own imagination to dance and mimic how they think the animal would dance. Here is a short sample list of animals you can call out and take a video of the dancing too!

Elephant, dog, cat, horse, cow, bull, sheep, goat, snake, dolphin, bear, spiders, platypus, rabbits, hyenas, lions, cheetahs, antelope, giraffe, gorilla, etc.

This dance game helps kids learn more about animals and gets their minds off themselves by watching the others dance. Use music from the Jungle book or whatever you choose. Instrumental songs are the best like "The Baby Elephant's Walk" or any instrumental song you like. You should see very interesting animal dancing movements!

Balloon juggle dancing. This helps their coordination. Give each child a balloon and tell them once the music starts, they need to lightly toss the balloon in the air and dance. While dancing they need to keep their balloon up in the air and prevent it from hitting the ground. The winner is the child or children whose balloons haven't hit the ground when the music stops. Try playing a fast tune then a slow tune.

Crazy Jumping Energy Expender Dance. This dance should get their energy out. Try an upbeat song like "Jump" by Van Halen> https://www.youtube.com/watch?v=SwYN7mTi6HM

Or any song you like. (Slow tunes are fun too if you tell them they must dance in slow motion).

For upbeat tunes like "Jump" tell the kids when the music starts, they need to jump (pick a safe area) and do the craziest, funniest, weirdest, jumping they can imagine.

This game also promotes creativity and quick thinking.

Impromptu Emotion Dancing. This helps their awareness of others and builds their vocabulary. Write down these emotions on slips of paper and put them in a bowl. Here is only a sample list of the many emotions people have,

Happy, Sad, Serious, Silly, Angry, Calm, Fear, Disgust, Surprise, Joy, Agony, Awkward, Clueless, Tired, Excited, Annoyed, Foolish, Crazy, Brainy, Stiff, Nervous, Free, Giddy, Bashful, Embarrassed, Brave, Sensitive, Shocking, Heartbroken, Bored, Lazy, Loving, Hesitant, Humiliated, Carefree, etc.

Play music and pick an emotion out of the bowl and hold it up so the kids can see it and say it out loud.

The kids take turns dancing to what they feel best shows the emotion. Call out another emotion for the next child and so on. Keep changing the emotions. You should see very interesting dance routines and take a movie!

DISABILITIES OR SPECIAL NEEDS ACTIVITIES

Make sure you've consulted with the child's medical provider before any activity. Be sure the activity does not contradict the medical professional's advice. The following are only suggestions, subject to what the child's medical provider recommends for activities.

Animals, Zoos, Animal Trainers. If you know your child or grandchild enjoys animals take them to a local farm or zoo. Or, visit a local animal breeder and check out the puppies, kittens, etc. Or, try a visit to a local dog trainer who would be willing to show you and the child what he or she does to train animals.

Animal Shelters. Petfinder.com has a list of local animal shelters where they treat and care for injured animals and nurse them back to health. Most every animal lover enjoys seeing the caring for injured animals. > https://www.petfinder.com/animal-shelters-and-rescues/search/

Fire Stations. If he or she likes fire trucks, most local fire stations will be happy to give a free tour. Most likely a Dalmatian will be there.

Hot Air Ballooning. This site has a list of organizations that offer hot air ballooning experiences for children with special needs. http://www.blastvalve.com/Balloon_Rides/Special_Needs/

Police Stations. Local police stations have been known to provide an opportunity for a tour of their police station. If a disabled child wants to see a police station, call with your local police station to see if they can show your disabled child around and give you a short tour.

Trainspotting is a train lover who has a keen interest in railways and railroads. If your child or grandchild likes trains, go to a local train station and talk to them about tours. If you are lucky, a staff member might show you the train station operation.

Aviation. If your child or grandchild likes aviation, visit your local small airport(s) which usually is far more interesting than large commercial airports. Most fixed-based operators at private or municipal airports love to show the facility to interested people. There also may be local flying clubs located there and a club member may take you up for a flight to show you and your child or grandchild a bird's eye view of your environment. Or, there may be other free or low-cost aviation opportunities that are unforgettable. See also the things listed in the first chapter of this book for more on aviation activities.

Greenhouses are great during cold winter to visit and to see how they operate year-round. And, they are fun to visit almost any time of the year. If you are in the New York area, there are nine amazing indoor gardens to visit where you can get out of the cold and enjoy the beauty of very large indoor gardens. https://theculturetrip.com/north-america/usa/new-york/articles/9-beautiful-indoor-gardens-to-visit-in-nyc/

Botanic Gardens. The Conservation International site provides information on local indoor gardens and spectacular outdoor gardens in many places throughout the world. https://www.bgci.org/

Kid Calisthenics. Star jumps are great and fun. Kids with autism may respond well to star jumps.[11] Star jumps begin with knees bent in a squat position then jumping up and out extending both arms and legs out as far as possible, then in one motion bringing their arms and legs back to the original starting position. Check out this site for kids with autism>
https://www.healthline.com/health/exercises-for-kids-with-autism#1.-Bear-crawls

Slamming a medicine ball. In this exercise, the child picks up a medicine ball of a suitable weight they can easily handle. Then they raise the ball up above their head and slam it to the floor! You can increase the weight as they get better.

Exercise videos. There are many exercise videos and calming techniques on YouTube for disabled or special needs children. The National Center on Health, Physical Activity and Disability (NCHPAD) has a 10-minute exercise video for children with autism > https://www.youtube.com/watch?v=PLoiHph_xwI

Build confidence. Kids with special needs or disabled kids prefer any activity they are somewhat good at it. It builds their confidence and may lead to increased social interaction opportunities. The goal is to increase their confidence and being good at something – no matter how simple or complex it may be!

Blind children. For visually impaired children, there are many things to do such as reading aloud, listening to audiobooks, and joining other visually impaired children's groups.

Listening to music, visiting a petting zoo, or visiting the park and feeling a plant and its roots, unusual bark of a tree, or exploring a museum with many sculptures and statutes is entertaining.

Creating your own sand sculpture at the beach or creating a sculpture with dry clay (playdough) enhances their creative abilities.

For vocal activities, sing karaoke, sing with the radio, etc. Do dancing games or try musical instruments.

Check to see if there is an aquarium near you with a hands-on section.

AD/HD Activities - Perform a script. Acting out a script gives AD/HD kids a way to express themselves and learn social skills. This site has movie scripts to read, choose a part, and perform as best as you can. https://www.lifehacker.com.au/2019/05/read-movie-scripts-with-your-kid/

AD/HD Legos. AD/HD kids learn motor skills and how to put ideas into reality building something and Legos is a simple and very popular way to get them interested.

Kids with AD/HD - Teach them photography. Show them how to use a camera and they will gain confidence and build their self-esteem when they create photos. See the DIRECTORY in the front of this book to find a chapter on Photography.

Kids with AD/HD - sports. Sports for kids with AD/HD are excellent since it provides a way of learning social skills and making new friends. It will build their self-esteem and confidence. The most important thing is to see if they enjoy the sport and if so, that's great even if they don't excel at it.

Asperger Syndrome - Drama classes. Kids with Asperger usually are intelligent kids with creativity. Acting out a script will help their communication skills. They will also make new friends in a drama class or drama playgroup.

Kids with Asperger and libraries and Legos. Many libraries have special interest groups where a child with Asperger can exercise his intellect and gain confidence and educate others. Most libraries welcome special kids to contribute new ideas to a library group to expand the minds of the other kids. Kids with Asperger also seem to enjoy building things and express themselves well with Legos.

Sites with events especially for kids with special needs. There are many sites with events for kids with special needs. Here are just a few and are growing all the time:

HUG> https://helpusgather.org/children-special-needs/

Chicago Parent for kids with special needs > https://www.chicagoparent.com/learn/special-needs/special-needs-events-to-get-on-your-calendar/

Support for families with special needs kids> https://www.supportforfamilies.org/special-family-events

Special needs kids' events in the Detroit area https://www.supportforfamilies.org/special-family-events

Events in New York for kids with special needs https://www.nymetroparents.com/article/inclusive-activities-and-events-for-kids-with-sensory-issues-and-special-needs-in-new-york-city-and-boroughs

EDUCATIONAL SCREEN STUFF – BRIGHT AND INTRIGUING

There are many Educational sites available to children. Keep in mind, the American Academy of Pediatrics and other child experts suggest only one to two hours of screen time a day for children ages 2 to 5 (i.e., screen time includes TV, surfing the net, video games, etc.). Older kids should have a balance. [12]

Kids might not have seen the following sites before, and all these sites involve educational screen activities.

Most kids already have favorite games they play all the time which makes it hard to give them educational substitute games. But these educational games have been very popular and most all are free.

CODESPARK Academy. This may seem too difficult for younger kids but if they enjoy and create using Minecraft, they can learn the basics of writing code with this free app. Many have been surprised at how popular this has become with kids. This site may charge fees for their courses.

Khan Academy Kids. Khan Academy is very well recognized for their excellent learning games for kids. Kids can learn reading, language, math, logic, and more. Most are free > https://www.khanacademy.org/kids

PBS KIDS. All of these are free, educational, and new games are introduced continually. https://pbskids.org/games/

Starfall. Starfall is a large educational site for kids. www.starfall.com

> **"It's weird. All those parenting books my wife made me read. And not one ever hinted that I have to remind my son not to touch the dog's but hole." – Jr. Williams**

EVENING FUN ACTIVITIES

For Grandparents - Skype Grandparents and vice-versa! A nice activity for the evening or weekends is to Skype and let grandparents know all is good with the precious ones and a chance for the kids to share what they did during the day. Vice-versa too if the kids are visiting grandparents.

Hand and Foot Massages. Hand and foot massages help them relax in the evening especially a half-hour before bedtime. There are also numerous videos online to show you how to do hand and foot massages on children. Here is a site showing foot massages> https://www.wikihow.com/Give-a-Foot-Massage

Set a time for going to bed. This will help make the kids understand evening fun will come to end at a certain time, so they won't keep playing past an agreed bedtime.

You can also set a time for getting ready for bed by scheduling a relaxing warm bath for them followed by getting into pajamas, picking out a bedtime storybook, a stuffed animal to take to bed, etc.

Evening swim. If there is an indoor swimming pool or aquatic center nearby, a relaxing half-hour or one-hour swim in the evening is beneficial for expending energy and may help get them ready for bedtime.

Invite adult friends to evening dinner. Inviting other adults (with no kids) for dinner will give the kids new opportunities to slow down and express themselves to others plus giving you a break for a while.

Appreciation time for you. Children at times can take parents and grandparents for granted. Ask them during quiet evening time what they most like about you as parents or grandparents. Tell them you are asking them this since you value their opinion very much. Tell them why you appreciate them too.

Camping out in the family room. Pitch a tent and have them create their own overnight camp in the family room. Have them sleep on air mattresses, assemble their favorite bedtime books, etc. It's easier than pitching a tent in the yard since the bathrooms are more available indoors.

Reading aloud and acting out stories. Choose a book and go heavy on voice inflections, changing voices and animated movements when you read the story. If they can read, take turns reading aloud and acting out each story. If a child or grandchild hasn't learned to read yet, suggest they tell a story about whatever they like and ask them to act it out. Capture it all on video.

Jigsaw puzzles. Jigsaw puzzles may tone them down a notch or two. Start with easy ones with large images. Put it aside for the second evening, and so on.

Coloring books and reading books. Coloring books allow the kids to focus on coloring and tones them down. Reading a great kid's book or a young adult book has the same effect.

Act out the "Kids Theatre." In the next chapter (Indoor activities) we suggest having the kids write a theatre play to show their playwriting abilities, and have the parents or grandparents act it out later.

If the kids wrote a play, you may want to act it out after dinner for them. It's a lot of laughs and the kids can see their own creations come to life. See this YouTube (over 5 million views) with Tom Hanks and Jimmy Fallon acting out plays written by elementary school kids where the kids were only given the title "Bridge of Spies," and the kids wrote a play about it. > https://www.youtube.com/watch?v=0p1Iv9z8bOY

In the next chapter, we also suggest how to have your kids write their own children's books with the parents or grandparents acting it out. The evening may be a great time to act this out as well.

Star Gazing. Check out free star viewing apps which will point out the names of stars, planets, and other nighttime sky information. You simply point your phone or pad at the sky and the names of the objects in the nighttime sky appear on the screen. For example, see these six apps for nighttime sky viewing with information> https://weloveweather.tv/top-6-astronomy-apps/

Or, see this Skyview app which will automatically name stars and constellations, as well as other objects in the sky > https://coolmomtech.com/2016/06/skyview-stargazing-app-cool-free-app-week/.

The child may like astronomy and continue his astronomical education which may become his livelihood or a lifetime hobby.

Catching fireflies. Catching fireflies is an old-fashioned evening activity time that kids love especially when they decide to see who can catch the most fireflies in a jar. Release them when you're done.

Evening night walk. A simple evening walk at night is an interesting thing for a child who doesn't often go for walks in the evening. The night world is different, very quiet and dark. Weather permitting, go for a walk around the block with everyone in their robes and pajamas. Take the dog too!

Board games. Board games are fun when played in the evening if they have had an active day. Pictionary, Charades, Dominoes, Chess, etc. are great evening games.

Establish an evening routine. Here is a sample evening routine as a guide to making up your own if you haven't got one already,

- Help with the dishes.
- Help with kitchen cleanup.
- Make their own lunch for the next day.
- Pick up all toys around the house.
- Talking about the day and plans for the next day.
- Getting ready for bed.

Evening hugs before bedtime. Just before bedtime, share hugs and good words to keep their moods positive, happy and relaxed.

INDOOR OR RAINY DAY FUN

Kids Theatre. Suggest the kids each write their own theatre play and the parents, or grandparents, will act it out. Give them only the title to the play like "Bridge of Spies" or "The Deer Hunter" or "On the Waterfront" or whatever you come up with. It's a lot of laughs if the kids write it up and the adults act it out. See this video (over 5 million views) with Tom Hanks and Jimmy Fallon acting out plays written by elementary school kids where the kids were only given the title "Bridge of Spies," and they had to write the rest. > https://www.youtube.com/watch?v=0p1Iv9z8bOY

Your kids or grandkids should all join in and collaborate writing the play on a rainy morning or afternoon and tell them you will act it out after dinner. See this adult site (which older kids may understand) which shows step by step how to write a theatre play. Or, you may want to explain to them how to do it in more simple terms. > https://www.wikihow.com/Write-a-Play-Script

Take a trip to the local museum or aquarium. Children wonder at and learn many things in museums and aquariums and can spend hours doing so. Many of these institutions have special sections for children. Look for exhibits where the kids can draw or make something.

Here are suggestions from the Smithsonian on what to do with kids in museums> https://americanhistory.si.edu/kids/kids-things-do-museum

Bowling with gutter guards. If your local lanes can install gutter guards, very young kids have a lot of fun bowling and it is great fun to introduce them to a great game they can enjoy for a lifetime.

Indoor skating rinks. Indoor roller skating or indoor ice-skating rinks are a lot of fun and great social opportunities for children.

Indoor pools. Always fun on rainy days and great exercise.

Family movies. Make popcorn and bring out old family videos!

Local movie theatres. Popcorn and a great movie!

Family board games. Monopoly, Scrabble, and other classic board games can strengthen family relationships.

Make a hideaway indoor fort. Kids love to make their own tent with towels, chairs, tables, etc. Have them construct it and give them a flashlight too with their favorite books, board games, etc.

Find the treat. Dogs smell 100 times better than humans and you and your kids or grandkids can have a lot of fun with this. If you have a dog, have the kids hide the dog's favorite treat in hideaway places around the home. Have the kids make a video of themselves hiding the dog treats. Then the video cameraman or kids should follow the dog finding the hidden treat. Ask the kids to keep trying different spots.

Dancing. See our Chapter on "Dancing Games" in this book for having lots of fun with dancing games indoors.

Magic shadows. Make shadow figures on the wall. Darken the room and use a flashlight and show them how to make shadow shapes on the wall. See this site for details and ideas > https://www.wikihow.com/Make-Shadow-Puppets

Playing cards. Old Maid, War, Go Fish, or any game you played when you were small. Remember Crazy 8's?

Ask kids to write a children's book. The younger you are the more imagination you have. If the kids like children's books, ask them to write a children's book. They should know from their own experience with children's books how to write one. Encourage them to be creative and make their own story up. Give them a notebook and colored pencils to begin. Act the story out in the evening and bring it to life!

Baking. Think back on how your mom taught you to bake. They love to watch the pastry dough rise and will love to eat it too! Decorate cupcakes with funny faces, googly cherry eyes, a chocolate galore celebration on top with a candle, a bright sprinkles star, a cupcake snowman, etc.

Make a paper airplane. Very simple and it teaches the children about air pressure, the principle of aerodynamic wing lift where the wing creates more lift than the weight of the plane. The child can adjust and experiment with plane design.

Have races and see who can design the plane that goes the farthest in distance. This site has some very interesting paper airplane designs>
https://www.diynetwork.com/made-and-remade/learn-it/5-basic-paper-airplanes

Reading aloud with your kids will help them succeed. Scientific studies have shown reading to your children will help them succeed better in school and will help them develop intellectual empathy. In other words, reading aloud increases the odds they will be more successful in life since it will help them quickly recognize how other people will react in situations. [13]

Read stories from children's picture books to kids 3-5. Research has also shown very young children who are read stories from picture books learn to read faster and associate objects with words faster as well as being exposed to one million words more than children who are not read to. [14]

Reading aloud to any child. Generally, older children who can read are not read to very often. Try to add drama, character voice changes, and voice inflections or invite them to read a story aloud.

Read a screenplay together aloud. Read a screenplay together and act out a scene. This site and others have well-known drafts of screenplays and acting one out can turn into a very enjoyable and memorable event. https://www.simplyscripts.com/movie-scripts.html

Read books. Read a book to young kids or have them read to themselves their favorite book. Kids have a tremendous amount of energy and it may be difficult to keep them in one place and read. Give it a try for 20-30 minutes and see what happens.

Parents.com has a page entitled, "18 Genius Ways to Make Kids Love Reading" and this article shows you 18 tricks to get the kids reading on their own. Check this out here> https://www.parents.com/toddlers-preschoolers/development/reading/18-genius-ways-to-make-kids-love-reading/

Legos. Legos are usually a lot of fun when it's raining outside and a way for kids or grandkids to express their creativity and many other skills.

Make puppets. Make puppets out of socks and help them create their own character with buttons for eyes, etc. See more detail here > https://www.wikihow.com/Make-a-Sock-Puppet

Grannie's Jewelry Box. Mom's or grandma's jewelry box is very appealing. Usually, grandma's is even more interesting to granddaughters than Mom's as grandma may have many stories on how she acquired a piece of jewelry over the years. The when, where, and why stories around a piece of jewelry are something they will remember whenever they see the piece of jewelry.

Observe your granddaughters as she goes through your jewelry and make a mental note if they are particularly interested in one or more pieces for a gift later. Take a photo of your granddaughters wearing a piece of your jewelry or take a movie of this precious time.

Dress up. A closet adventure in mom's, dad's, grandma's or grandpa's closet is a lot of fun, of course. Take pictures and show them at family events when they are grown.

Child Meditation. Learning meditation can make a person healthier in the hectic world of today and it may be something very useful in future years. There are numerous videos on helping kids learn meditation which is fun to learn on a dreary rainy day. Check this out> https://www.youtube.com/watch?v=Bk_qU7l-fcU

JOKE TELLING TIME

"Laughing together is a way to connect, and a good sense of humor also can make kids smarter, healthier, and better able to cope with challenges." - Dr. Mary L. Gavin, M.D.

Kids love to tell jokes and share them with their friends like,

Boy: The principal is really stupid!

Girl: Ah...do you know who I am?

Boy: No... Who are you?

Girl: I am the principal's daughter!

Boy: Ah...Okay! Now I know who you are.

Do you know who I am?

Girl: No.

Boy: (walks away)

Telling Riddles and Jokes. Have a joke contest. Have each child take a turn to tell their favorite joke and have everyone vote whose joke they liked the best. Have two out of three or three out of five contests so if they don't win with the first joke they can try again. Use a microphone if you have one and encourage them to stand while telling jokes to improve their confidence and develop their public speaking skills.

Riddles can be shared and solved by the whole family trying to find the answer. Ask your children or grandchild to tell you a riddle they might know. See the samples in the next paragraph.

Sample Jokes and Riddles. These samples are from our books, "Jokes for Very Funny Kids (Ages 3-7) and "Jokes for Very Funny Kids (Big & Little)."

Do butterflies fart? When you see a butterfly do this and you immediately know the butterfly just farted. What is it?

Answer. It flys in a straight line for a few seconds!

*

How do you train a Matta-ewe? (sheep)

What's a Matta-ewe?

Nothing. Whatsamattayou?

*

An impatient man in a restaurant asks the waiter, "Waiter, how long will my pizza be?"

The waiter said, "Not very long, sir... It will be shaped like a circle."

*

Q. How do you know if your dog is slow?

A. He chases parked cars!

*

Q. Why do giraffes have long necks?

A. Because they have smelly feet!

*

Q. Why do monkeys have big noses?

A. Because they have big fingers!

*

Try acting out this next joke while telling it imitating the blind man,

A blind man with a seeing-eye dog went into a large department store. He walked to the middle of the store and picked up the dog and kept moving around and around turning his dog this way and that and moving the dog up and down.

The salespersons didn't know what was going on since they hadn't ever seen anything like this before. The manager of the store approached the blind man and said, "Excuse me. May I help you with something?"

The blind man said, "No thanks. I'm just looking around."

*

Here's another funny one to act out,

A store was having a big sale and lowered all their prices by 75%. Word spread throughout the city the store was selling everything at a very low price. Hundreds of people were lined up by the front door waiting for the store to open. Many of them had been waiting 8 hours or more so they could get in the store first before the others and buy all the greatest bargains.

An old man kept trying to get to the front of the line, but he was pushed back many times. He still tried very hard to get to the front of the line when a large man picked him up, carried him to the back of the line, and threw him on the ground.

"That's it," said the old man. "One more time I get pushed out; I'm not going to open my store!"

*

Mom announced, "These veggies will give you the vitamins your bodies need!"

"Yes, we know that Mom!" The children replied.

"And who serves them on your plate at dinner time at just the right temperature?" Mom asked.

"You do Mom!"

"And who steams these beautiful and colorful veggies to preserve all the vitamins in them!"

"You do Mom!" The children replied.

"And who works very hard to get the money to buy these marvelous and nutritious veggies!"

"Dad does!" The children replied.

Mom: "Then why don't you eat them?"

"We don't like them, Mom!"

*

Dad asks, "Joey do you think I'm a bad father?"

Son says, "My name is George."

*

Dad: "Son, you should not drink any alcoholic beverages."

Son: "But Dad, you drink beer?"

Dad: "Yes, that's right son. But I'm not an alcoholic."

Son: "What's an alcoholic?"

Dad: "Well you see those 4 cars over there. An alcoholic would see 8 cars instead of 4 cars."

Son: "Ah...Dad, there are only 2 cars over there."

*

Joe didn't like his little brother Johnny since Dad seemed to give Johnny his way all the time. Joe decided to talk to his Dad about it.

"Dad, why do you give Johnny his way all the time! All he has to do to get his way is to walk back and forth screaming at the top of his lungs, then sit in a chair crying and crying for what he wants!"

"Yes, I do that with Johnny. That's because Johnny is going to be a great basketball coach someday!"

*

Grandma and Grandpa attended Church on a Sunday morning and grandma leaned over to grandpa and said, "I'm sorry, but I just let out a long, silent fart."

"That's okay, but you'd better get the batteries in your hearing aid replaced!"

*

Three-year-old Joey sat next to a pregnant woman in Church and quietly asked her why she looked so fat.

"I have a baby inside me," the woman whispered.

"Is it a good baby?"

"Yes, it is a *very* good baby," the woman said.

"Then why did you eat it?!"

*

A young man saw a woman in the grocery store with her two-year-old daughter riding in the grocery cart. As they passed the cookie section, the two-year-old girl pointed to the cookies, but her mother said no. The little girl began to throw a big tantrum and started to scream, shout and cry.

The mother said, "Now Jane, there are only two aisles to go and don't be upset."

Then they passed the chocolate section and the little girl pointed at the chocolate and the mother kept on wheeling past it. The little girl again began to scream and shout for chocolate.

"Now Jane," the mother said, "there's just one aisle to go and don't be upset. It won't be too long now."

Then they passed a toy section right before the checkout and the little girl pointed to the toys. The mother passed the toys, and the little girl again screamed and shouted. Everyone in the store could hear her.

"Now Jane, we'll be out of here soon and when we get home you can have a nap. Be patient, it won't be long now." The mother said.

A man who was watching all this went up to the woman and said, "I have to admire you. You are so patient your little daughter, Jane."

The mother interrupted, "My little girl's name is Mary...I'm Jane."

*

Three-year-old Joey told his mom his stomach hurt.

"That's because your stomach is empty. You should put something in it," Mom replied.

The next day, Dad brought his boss over for dinner who said before he sat down, "I'm sorry but do you have any aspirin? My head hurts."

"That's because it's empty," Joey said. "You should put something in it."

*

Here are more examples of riddles for the whole family to solve from our book "Jokes for Very Funny Kids (Big & Little)" (also, check out the Brainbuster Riddles Chapter in this book for difficult riddles for the whole family to solve. The answers to these difficult riddles are in the back of this book). Here are simple ones.

Q. What is it that poor people possess, rich people need, and if you eat it, you will eventually die?

A. Nothing.

*

A woman is in her hotel room. She hears someone knocking on the door. She gets up and opens the door and immediately sees a very well-dressed man she doesn't know.

The well-dressed man is very polite and says, "Oh, I made a mistake. I am very sorry. I thought this was my room."

The man turns and walks down the hallway to the elevator and goes down the elevator. The woman picks up her phone and calls security right away. Why did the woman call security?

A. A normal person would not knock on the door before going into his own hotel room.

*

A man asked the Director of a mental hospital how he determines if a patient is required to be admitted to the hospital.

"Well," said the Director, "We bring the patient over to a bathtub we've filled up with water. Then we give the patient an eyedropper, a tablespoon, a small teacup, and a very large bucket and ask the patient to get all of the water out of the bathtub."

The man said, "Oh, I understand! A normal person would choose the bucket since its larger. If they don't choose that, are they admitted to the hospital?

A. "No," said the Director. "Most normal people simply pull the plug."

"There are so many funny kids and teenagers. They're just not aware of how funny they are." - Vanessa Bayer

LIBRARY ADVENTURES

Look for the biggest book. Search for the biggest book in the Library and once you find the biggest book take a photo of the kids standing next to it.

Research recipes in cookbooks. Find one or two interesting recipes from your family's ethnic background and plan to cook it together. Irish stew? Italian Lasagna?

Rainy day reading. Introduce your kids or grandkids to your local library and read a book to them from the children's section. Have them select the book. Or, choose it yourself if they can't agree on a book, or ask each to choose a book and read them.

Audiobook section. Most libraries have an audiobook section and introduce them to audiobooks and the procedures in your local library to listen to them if they don't have an audio player. If they are familiar with audiobooks, have them explore while you relax.

Find the "How to draw" books section. Find "How to Draw" books. Kids love to learn how to do a drawing of a cat or dog or whatever interests them. Bring a pencil and paper or ask the librarian for pencils and paper.

Children's book clubs. Your library may have a children's book club where they can socialize with others and share the joy of reading. See if your kids or grandkids would like to join a club.

Teach them how to check out books, and eBooks, etc. Introduce them to the local librarian and have them learn a free source of books on any subject that interests them such as games, sports, children's jokes, knock-knock jokes, dad jokes, riddles, tongue twisters, different countries, etc.

Ask the librarians for their recommendations on what children's books are more popular than others – it might surprise you!

Ask the librarian to give you and your children or grandchildren a tour of the library for their future reference.

Newspaper & Magazine Section. If they are older, they might want to explore recent news. Show them how and generally explore the library slowly to see what interests them. Be sure to show them the reference section since the reference books will help them with homework, after school projects, etc.

Future Writers. Most libraries will have information on children's writing contests where the children can develop their writing talents if they have an interest in becoming a writer. Keep in mind, some children who may not verbalize themselves very well because of social anxiety, or other reasons, are sometimes very gifted and creative writers.

Kids love to create their own illustrated children's books which is great fun for them and a great exercise for their imagination. The "How to Draw" books will help them.

Travel Section. The travel section of a library will expand their knowledge about the world where they can learn at their own pace.

Future Chefs and more cookbooks. The library might have a cooking/recipe book section where they can explore how to make things like their own cakes and even ice cream. Most importantly they can learn healthy recipes. They also can learn many variations of recipes for their favorite foods and different ways of preparing foods for breakfast, lunch, and dinner!

Quotations, Poetry. Introduce them to quotation books and poetry for inspiration, motivation, and intriguing thoughts to help them expand their lives and thinking.

Have fun in the reference section. Find the child's favorite reference book. Ask the kids or grandkids to look up the meaning of their own name and the meanings of the names of their family and friends.

Computers. If they aren't already computer savvy, most libraries allow the use of computers for limited time periods. Show the child how to use these or ask the librarian to explain their computer use system.

MAGIC TRICKS FOR LITTLE WIZARDS

Magic freezing water. Place and wedge a small sponge at the bottom of a cup and place an ice cube on top of the dry sponge. Pour a small amount of water into the cup. Say the magic word, e.g., "Freezerino!". Then pick up the cup and pour out the ice cube! Teach this and the other tricks to your children or grandchildren. They will love it and will share it with their friends!

Magic pre-sliced banana in its own peel. When no one is watching, use a pin to horizontally slice a banana in its peel by sticking the pin in equidistant points along the banana and moving it sideways to slice the inside of the banana in roughly equal-sized slices while the banana is still inside its peel. Then, replace the banana in a fruit bowl.

When the kids or grandkids come in, nonchalantly take the banana from the bowl. Tell them you can magically slice the banana in pieces for all to share. Show them the banana so they will see that it looks like an ordinary banana. Wave your hand over the banana and say a magic word (e.g., "Slicerino!") then pretend to slice it horizontally with your fingers.

Slowly peel the banana to reveal the slices already in the banana and share it with them.

Find the chosen card. Prearrange a deck of playing cards so that all the red cards are on top of the deck and all the black cards are at the bottom of the deck.

Holding the cards face down so that you cannot see them, fan out a few cards from the top of the deck (they will be the red cards) and ask your child or grandchild to pick a card from the few cards you fanned out at the top of the deck. Ask them to remember the card.

Then fan out a few cards from the bottom of the deck and ask your child or grandchild to replace the card they just picked back into the deck where you have fanned out cards from the bottom.

Then roughly split the deck in half placing the bottom half on top of the deck. Lift up and fan out the cards to yourself (so no one else can see them) and pick out the red card which should be the only red card amongst the black cards. Pull out the card and ask, "Is this your card?" Viola! You are an amazing magician!

Remember to show your child or grandchild how you did this so he or she can show it to their friends!

Magic pepper repel. Before doing this trick rub soap from a bar of soap on your index finger.

Sprinkle pepper on the surface of a glass of water and ask the child to place their finger into the water and the pepper granules will simply continue to float on top without moving from the person's finger.

Then say the magic word (e.g., Pepperino!") and place your secretly soaped finger into the water. The pepper will magically disperse away from and separate from your finger.

Magically guess anyone's age. Ask the kids or grandkids or anyone to put in their age in a desk calculator without you seeing what they put in.

Then ask them to use the calculator and multiply it by 2.

Then ask them to add 1 to it.

Then ask them to multiply that result by 5.

Then ask them to multiply that number by 10.

Then ask them to write the answer down on a piece of paper.

You then look at the number on the paper and ignore the last two digits. The number which is left is the age of the person!

Read minds! Magically guess any number! Ask one of your kids or grandkids to think of a number from 1 to 9 and not to tell you what it is (asking them to pick a number between 1 and 9 is easier for a child to do the math which follows).

Then ask the child to multiply the number by 2.

Then ask the child to multiply the result by 5.

Then ask the child to write down the result on a piece of paper.

You look at the paper and disregard the zero at the end of their result and that is the number they thought of.

For example, say someone picks the number 4. They multiply that by 2 which is 8. Then they multiply the 8 by 5 which comes to 40. You disregard the zero and the number they originally chose was 4.

4 x 2 = 8.

8 x 5 = 40.

Drop the zero and the number 4 is left (their chosen number).

You can also do this with much higher numbers, but the person may need a calculator to do the multiplication by 2 and then multiplying that result by 5.

For example, say you asked the person to think of any number and the person thought of 5,489 as their number.

5,489 x 2 = 10,978

10,978 x 5 = 54,890. You drop the zero at the end and that is their original number – 5489!

The magical number 37! Ask the child to think of a three-digit number where all the digits are the same (e.g., 111, 222, 777, etc.) Then ask the child to add the three digits together (e.g. 1+1+1=3). Then ask the child to divide the three-digit number by the sum of the three digits added together (111/3=37). The answer is always 37 with any three digit number where all the digits are the same!

Many other magic tricks. There are 7 magic tricks on this site that take practice, but they amaze children and they will call you a true magician if you do them. Teach these tricks to them too so they can amaze their friends > https://www.wikihow.com/Do-Easy-Card-Tricks

MEMORIES – PRESERVING THEM

Digital Scrapbooking. Digital scrapbooks are great since there is no need for glue, you can add pages and pages, edit anytime and update as you wish. You can do this on your computer or buy special programs to assist you. Kids and grandkids can most likely assist you with it too. You can add animations and music as well. Here is a link for beginners to create your own digital scrapbook and perhaps your kids or grandkids might want to watch how you do this and make one too! > https://www.wikihow.com/Create-a-Digital-Scrapbook

Instagram or other Photo Printing. There are many companies like Social Print Studios and others that will print your photos from your Instagram Account. You simply select the photos you want to be printed and send them to a printing company and receive great photos. Some companies will print the photos you send them and put them in a book as well. Google to find the many social print companies online that will create a personal memory book for you to create from your photos and share with your kids, grandkids, great-grandkids, etc.

Establish a tradition to strengthen bonds. One way to be remembered well is to have a family tradition that you instituted. If your kids or grandkids enjoy fishing, take them on an annual fishing trip.

If the kids or grandkids love a certain dish you make (e.g., your special meatballs, lasagne or cook whatever they look forward to when they visit), teach them how to make it and write the recipe down for them titled under your name.

Find out what each enjoys the most and establish a tradition of doing that every time they visit or every time annually.

Examples of family traditions are varied and could be anything you initiate for the family such as a cooking a favorite dish, making a special Sunday morning breakfast, a secret handshake, creating a special way of doing family hugs, family singing times, family game night, making up a family time capsule and burying it where your family will have access to it in future years, telling a story on a special occasion like Christmas or Thanksgiving, having a family dance party, walks on evenings with full moons, etc.

Tell them about yourself, Grandparents. Tell grandkids who may not know the details of your life, what you like to do the most and why. Tell them stories about yourself and show them what kind of person you are. Your stories will be remembered well. As Jim Henson once said, "Kids don't remember what you try to teach them. They remember what you are."

Help the world and talk about it. If you are helping the world in small ways, tell your kids and grandkids about it. For example, are you are a volunteer at the local hospital or a member of a group trying to correct the environment? Tell them your reasons for doing good work. Show them your giving and kindness by your example and your unconditional love for them. They will remember what you did for the rest of their lives.

For Grandparents. A reminder and ways to make grandchildren feel special and needed. Give your grandchildren small tasks to help you do something you "just can't do yourself" such as getting dead leaves out of corner places in the garden, or cleaning small hard to reach places in your home, or cutting flowers and putting them in a vase, or doing something you just can't get around to doing. You can ask them questions about an app or a laptop issue you might have or anything you know they are knowledgeable about. Tell them how much you appreciate their help and how important they are to you. They will remember you for that.

Record your story with them and store it on StoryCorps.org. Have the kids or grandkids interview you and record it. You can help prepare questions for your grandchildren to interview you on your life and preserve your personal story on Storycorps.org > https://storycorps.org.

MINUTE TO WIN IT GAMES

LOL Minute to Win It Games. These games are very popular with kids and originated from an international game show franchise.

The games involve 60-second challenges using objects commonly found around the home. The games are a lot of fun and laughs and are relatively simple. When one challenge is completed the participants go on to the next challenge.

For example, two kids can race to see who can knock the most paper cups off a table by blowing up a balloon and expelling the air in the balloon to blow the cups of the table. This requires blowing up the balloon several times.

There are hundreds of different "Minute to Win It" games – too many to list in this book. For example, here is a site with a large assortment of minute to win it games > https://toodrie.com/minute-to-win-it-games-for-teens/

OUTDOOR ADVENTURES – WONDERS OF NATURE

Avoiding "Nature Deficit Disorder." Author Richard Louv first wrote in 2005 that many kids suffer from obesity, higher rates of emotional illness, physical illnesses and other problems due to spending too much time on-screen.

Further research by others tends to show Nature Deficit Disorder contributes to a diminished use of senses and focusing difficulties. [15]

Richard Louv and many others recommend more outdoor activities for a well-balanced and healthier child.

Feeling tree bark. If you are in a wooded area, blindfold your child or grandchild and take the child by the hand using a zig-zag route to a tree with heavy and somewhat unique bark. Have the child feel the bark of the tree for a minute or so taking in as much detail as he or she can.

Go back to where you started and remove the blindfold and ask the child to locate the tree. This exercise will enlighten the child on the contours and wonders of trees.

Then put the blindfold on yourself and let the child test you to see if you can locate a tree. They will love it! Do this several times with different trees.

Summer berry picking. Wild blackberries grow in the summer. Show your kids or grandkids how blackberries or other wild fruit grow from bushes. Pick a few berries, wash them and take them home. Watch out for thorns and as you probably know already, pick the ones at the top since animals, dogs, etc. may have peed on the lower ones.

Wildflower picking. This is a very simple activity, but if the children haven't ever done floral arrangements, you can teach them what to pick and take them home and teach them how to arrange the different flowers you found.

Tree growth rings. If you come across a stump or a log, show the child the annual growth rings of a tree and explain how the rings show how old the tree is since each ring represents one year.

Feed wild birds with breadcrumbs. If you have a birdwatcher's guide or any bird field guide, toss breadcrumbs out and see how many different birds land to eat them and identify them using your guide. The Audubon Society has a lot of information on how to get children interested in bird watching and other information on guides to identify the birds > https://www.audubon.org/news/easy-ways-get-kids-birding

Winter bird feeding. You may need a sturdy birdfeeder in your backyard in winter months to withstand severe weather. Wide covers and wide feeding platforms seem to work the best. Winter feeding in the backyard is best with sunflower seeds, peanuts, millet, and even peanut butter.

Find pinecones and tie a string to one end of each pinecone which you use to hang it from a tree limb. Before hanging a pinecone, smear peanut butter or honey on the outside of the pinecone and sprinkle it with birdseed or crumbs. Hang them outside and watch the birds find it. Take pictures/movies of the different birds who visit.

Many birds in the forest areas search for food in the winter and if you keep putting food out in the same spot in the forest, birds will watch for you. The National Wildlife Federation has more information on winter bird feeding > https://blog.nwf.org/2015/01/tips-for-winter-bird-feeding/

Start a campfire with a magnifying glass. First, check out any applicable fire restrictions in the area you choose to build a campfire. Build the fire on a rock base or another non-flammable base and surround it as well with rocks.

Show the kids how to find and make tinder, which are very light particles of birch bark, wood shavings, curling's, very dry leaf particles, etc. so that air can pass through quickly as the tinder heats from the magnifying glass. Explain how fires need air, i.e., oxygen to ignite. Oxygen is needed since the tinder has the chemical element of carbon in it and it is the carbon that burns and catches fire. This is because the increasing heat from the magnifying glass which focuses the sun's rays causes a chemical reaction with carbon and oxygen. This chemical reaction creates carbon dioxide. There is a great amount of heat from this chemical reaction which we commonly call "fire".

Keep a small pile of tinder and piles of very small sticks alongside with larger sticks and branches nearby to build the fire more and create good flames. Explain that the shape of a magnifying glass with its two-sided convex lens focuses the sun's rays into one single point which creates a great amount of heat needed to start the chemical reaction.

If you have trouble starting a campfire with a magnifying glass, you might want to check out this site for very detailed instructions> https://www.wikihow.com/Create-Fire-With-a-Magnifying-Glass

Have a water supply or proper fire extinguishing equipment nearby to extinguish the fire completely and show them how to extinguish the fire safely and not to leave the area until the fire is completely extinguished with absolutely no burning embers, and cool to touch with no chance of restarting.

Bring marshmallows too!

Pitch a tent or make a shelter. Kids love to make their own den or hideaway indoors with chairs and blankets in the home. Now that you are outdoors, show them how to pitch a small tent or make an outdoor shelter. There are numerous ways to build an outdoor shelter using only the native bush. For ideas on what might suit you best, check out this article on making shelters outside in the wilderness>
https://www.wikihow.com/Make-a-Shelter-in-the-Wilderness

Nature Photography and General Photography. Warn them against and watch out for any child looking directly into the sun. Make sure they know not to try to look at or take a photo of the sun. Abandon photography if you think there is any possibility of anyone trying to take a picture of the sun. Focus on taking close-ups of flowers, plants, compositions of rocks, sand on beaches, snowflakes, insects, rain hitting puddles, etc. The list of the kinds of photographs they can take is limitless once they learn how to take a photo.

Close-up pictures of insects, especially beetles, spiders, etc., produce very interesting and amazing pictures. Also, close-ups of plants and grasses, turn into amazing photos when taken close. Show them how to develop a creative eye for photographs before snapping a photo.

The texture, shapes, and curves of a close-up of a simple earthworm, or tree bark, flowers, stems, roots, etc. can be great subjects for Composition Photography, i.e., photographs that show patterns, curves, lines, contrasts, etc. This leads to more fun when your children or grandchildren ask their friends if they can guess what's in the picture.

See the Photography chapter in this book which follows as well for more on photography.

Hiking and Exploring. If there are hiking trails available through the forest, try one or two out if they are not too grueling. Check the weather first.

Sing songs along the way like "The Ants Go Marching One by One" or "The Happy Wanderer," i.e., "I Love to Go a Wandering…" or any song you like.

When hiking, teach them about finding food sources or what is commonly referred to as "foraging." When hiking, show them how to forage and find foods on their own. See this very informative article on food foraging > https://www.wikihow.com/Forage-for-Food-in-the-Fall

Survival. We hope getting lost in the woods doesn't ever happen to you or your children or grandchildren but knowing what to do in a survival situation is valuable and something they will remember all their lives especially if they ever should need it. Here is a comprehensive site on survival in the wilderness if you ever get lost. It deals with finding water, building shelters, and more > https://www.wikihow.com/Survive-in-the-Woods.

Orientating. Briefly teach them about finding their directions in the forest. Explain how the sun rises in the East and sets in the West.

If it's cloudy, climb a tree to hopefully see distant landmarks off in the distance. If you find a stream, suggest most streams lead into rivers and people are usually living around rivers or fishing or recreating in rivers.

Another way to tell which way North is to observe the shape of anthills. Ants create anthills with a gradual slope pointing to the South and a steep slope pointing to the North.

Finally, explain how a compass works and tell them to remember when they enter a forest to remember what general direction they are walking and teach them how to use a compass.

A Lesson on Poison Ivy. Teach them about poison ivy and what to do if the bad itchy rash develops from contacting the poison ivy leaves. If it happens, use calamine lotion, cool compresses, and more information on how to treat poison ivy is in this Mayo Clinic video> https://www.mayoclinic.org/diseases-conditions/poison-ivy/diagnosis-treatment/drc-20376490

Bike Trails and Mountain Biking. Many forest preserves have interesting bike paths with rest stops along the way. For older kids, look for mountain biking trails which are a lot of fun and adventure. Mountain biking can be difficult and dangerous. But it is exhilarating!

"Restore balance. Most kids have technology, school and extracurricular activities covered. It's time to add a pinch of adventure, a sprinkle of green time and a big handful of play." - Penny Whitehouse

PHOTOGRAPHY

Time-lapse photography. If your camera has a time-lapse setting, see this site for an easy guide to the world of time-lapse photography - your phone camera may have it>https://www.wikihow.com/Shoot-Time-Lapse-Photography

Color or Alphabet Photography for small children. Ask the child to go outside (or inside the home) and (1) Take 3 photographs of things of a certain color, and (2) Take 3 photographs of things that begin with each letter of the alphabet as it helps small children learn colors and the alphabet.

Show them the basics of good photography. A person can spend a lifetime studying and learning about the vast world of photography. For children just starting out show them these rules (if they aren't aware of these basic rules already).

Fill the frame. If you are taking a photo of a very interesting subject show them how to fill the whole frame with the subject. This shows much more detail in the subject when taking a closeup.

Pointing or leading lines. If the background has several lines in one direction, try to position the subject so the lines point to the subject. By doing this, anyone viewing the photo will have their eyes automatically guided to the subject.

Cropping. Show them how to crop a photo. Tell them there is a basic rule not to chop off a bent limb at the joint of a person or a bent limb at the joint of an animal when cropping.

Rule of thirds. Each photo can be considered a work of art and to properly fill a frame most photographers use the "Rule of thirds." Imagine or adjust the camera so that it has a tic-tac-toe grid over it. This creates a guide to one-third of the picture both horizontally and vertically. The subject of the photo should be placed at an intersection or along one of the lines of the grid.

Window light. Position the subject by the window to show how window light gives more depth to the subject and creates shadows.

Start with an inexpensive camera. If your child wants to go further in photography, most camera stores recommend you start with an inexpensive camera. A zoom feature is good to have as well as rechargeable batteries.

Teach them to take candid photos. Most of the time, kids use the automatic mode and ask people to smile and pose. Teach them about taking candid photos to capture real feelings and emotions.

Learn more. If a child or grandchild has a growing interest in photography this site has many ways for your child or grandchild's to learn more about the photography world > https://www.wikihow.com/Category:Photography

"Taking pictures is like tiptoeing into the kitchen late at night and stealing Oreo cookies." – Diane Arbus

PIE IN THE FACE FUN

Whipped Cream Pie Spelling Bee. Tinfoil pie plates filled with whipped cream are messy, but kids will love it especially when you combine it with a spelling bee. Have the children sit around a table with each having a small tin pie plate filled with whipped cream in front of them. Have a can of whipped cream handy for refills.

Have a spelling bee where each child is asked a word to spell. If the child gets it wrong the child to the left will pick up the plate and gently push it into the face of the child who spelled it incorrectly. The game continues right or wrong.

Then it's the turn of the child to the left and if that child spells the word incorrectly, the child to the left that child will likewise gently push the tin plate in that child's face, and so on around the table.

Mom, dad, grandma and grandpa can play too which increases the laughter and memories!

The play continues for a set time or until you run out of whipped cream. Take movies, pictures, etc. Choose simple words to begin with so the tension will mount as they spell words correctly. Gradually increase the difficulty of the words to build even more tension. Most importantly, have fun!

Here is a sample list of easy words (please make up your own list suitable for the children).

Easy words to start with. See, the, door, any, both, do, fun, go, give, for, spell, run, dog, cat.

More difficult words. Know, lean, learn, chow, again, wrestle, although, answer, accept, marriage, patient, vault, vacuum, acquire, scissors, millionaire, lightning, vegetable.

Very difficult words. Language, different, neither, mammal, dolphin, journey, laughter, inventor, authority, competent, numeral, cuckoo, sizzle.

Very, very difficult words. Onomatopoeia, Milieu, conscientious, acquiescence, surveillance, precocious, unconscious, receive, mechanic, advantageous, souvenir, questionnaire.

Whipped cream math quiz. Instead of a spelling bee, you could use math questions by asking them simple additions, subtractions, divisions, and/or the multiplication table questions (7 x 8 equals what? - and so on). Chose math questions according to their ages and likewise increase the difficulty as you go along.

Find the jellybean in the pie. Have the kids sit down with their hands behind their back with a small tin pie plate that has 4 jellybeans at the bottom and fill the rest of the pie plate with whipped cream.

The first one to find and eat all 4 jellybeans without using their hands or fingers wins! Take a movie and replay it years later for lots of laughs. (Teens and adults enjoy this game too).

Apple bobs with no hands. Put several apples in a large flat bowl or pan and cover the apples with whipped cream. The game is played like bobbing for apples where the players try to get an apple using only their mouths. Take turns and take pictures and the person who gets the most apples in a set time (1 minute, etc.) is the winner.

Finish the bowl. Each child has a bowl in front of them filled with whipped cream. The object of the game is to see who can finish eating their bowl the fastest. Once a child finishes a bowl, he or she holds it up and inverts it over their head to show it is empty. The other players must immediately stop eating when the first child finishes and take their bowl and invert what's left in the bowl over their own head!

"Life's too short to skip the whipped cream." – Anon.

PIZZAS AND OTHER STUFF

Developing future chefs. Kids and grandkids love pizza. Learning how to make a pizza (as well as any other food item) helps develop their creative skills as well as improve their motor skills. They also learn teamwork and multitasking skills and introduces them to the culinary arts. It is something they will have for the rest of their life and will remember you taught them.

If they are experienced in making pizzas, challenge them to make a pizza with toppings they haven't made before!

How to make the basic pizza. Place dough on greased baking paper or pan, add sauce, a few toppings, cheese and place it in a preheated oven at 450 degrees F, for twenty minutes or until golden brown.

There are countless pizza recipes. Here are just a few topping combinations to try out on pizza dough already sauced,

- Broccoli and cheddar

- Thin sliced preboiled potatoes, oregano, parmesan cheese, and bacon
- Ham, cheddar, and apple slices
- Cheese, pineapple, and bacon
- Chicken, salami, and bacon
- Red onion, olives, capsicum, and BBQ sauce
- Crushed garlic, oregano, parmesan cheese, bacon and chipotle sauce
- Onion, sliced hotdogs, and mustard
- Spaghetti, ham, oregano and parmesan cheese.
- Blackberry, cheese and fennel pizza. These can be foraged. Wash them first since you know what dogs and other animals do on lower branches!

Strange and Unusual Pizzas. See this Thrillist.com site for very unusual pizzas recipes including a whole Lobster pizza > https://www.thrillist.com/eat/nation/strangest-pizza-toppings

Funny face pizzas. Let them use their imagination in creating a pizza with a replica of their own face or your face using olives for eyes, anchovy eyebrows, tomatoes for cheeks, a broccoli nose, green beans for lips, etc. Leave the toppings out for them and let them create it!

Other stuff. Here are a few quick suggestions for simple dishes kids seem to like.

Mom's or Grandma's Pita sandwich. Use raw or baked apple slices, or apple sauce with peanut butter and banana slices and put them in a pita pocket for a great pita sandwich!

Mom's or Grandma's Macaroons. These are easy to make. All you need are,

- 5 1/2 cups of sweetened shredded coconut

- 2-3 teaspoons of vanilla extract

- 14 oz. can sweeten condensed milk

- Jar of maraschino cherries.

Combine the coconut and condensed milk in a bowl and mix. Drop a tablespoon-sized ball of the mixture on a greased baking sheet, and place in a preheated 350 F oven for 10 to 12 minutes or until golden brown. Serve each macaroon with a maraschino cherry on top.

Teach Family recipes. Teach them a recipe your mother or grandmother taught you. Try to give them one for their favorite food they like to eat. Take photos. Write down the recipe for them and put the date on it.

Dishes for age groups. Teach them to make dishes appropriate for their present age > https://www.eatright.org/homefoodsafety/four-steps/cook/teaching-kids-to-cook

**"Cooking with kids is not just about ingredients, recipes, and cooking.
"It's about harnessing imagination, empowerment, and creativity."** – Guy Fieri

RAINING? THERE'S STILL A LOT OF FUN OUTSIDE!

If the rain isn't torrential, and there's no lightning, there are many things to do in the rain which are lots of fun.

Worm hunting. Worms come out in the rain and researchers aren't exactly sure why they do that. Some say worms have an instinct telling them they can travel easier on the ground when it rains. Others say worms feel the vibrations of the raindrops which instinctively makes them go to the surface. Birds have been observed pecking on the ground making vibrations to get worms to surface. In any event, if you plan to go fishing, worms are usually great bait for freshwater fish. If there is an evening rain, take a flashlight and bucket.

Jumping puddles and singing. Pick out different puddles and see who can jump over the largest puddle. Sing songs while the kids are enjoying the rain like, "Singing in The Rain," "It's Raining It's Pouring," "Raindrops Keep Falling on My Head," etc.

Make boats out of recyclables. See this interesting site which shows you how to make toy boats to sail in puddles out of recyclables > https://www.instructables.com/id/How-to-make-a-toy-boat-from-recycled-material/

Make a paper boat. See this site which shows you how to make toy boats to sail in puddles out of paper in step by step > https://www.wikihow.com/Make-a-Paper-Boat.

Make a cardboard boat. See this site to make a toy boat out of cardboard. The cardboard boat is one you may want to keep inside the home when it's too nasty to go outside> https://www.wikihow.com/Make-a-Cardboard-Ship

Homemade boat races. You can use your imagination and engineering skills to make small boats out of anything like popsicle sticks, plastic water bottle boats, or whatever the kids might come up with. See who can make the best-designed boat that will win a race in a flowing stream from a rain gutter. Or hold a race where the kids can only make waves without touching the boat to propel their boat.

If the kids have made sailboats, have a race where the kids propel their boats by blowing through straws or using the air in a balloon.

Or, see whose boat stays afloat the longest in the rain.

Blow bubbles in the rain. Most kids haven't tried this yet and it is LOL fun to see who can blow the biggest bubble before raindrops burst it.

Follow the rain. Teach the kids about gravity and the flow of water. Does it flow and empty into a drain? Or, does it go to a larger pond? Tell them how streets are engineered in order to have water flow downward to drains to prevent flooding.

Measuring rainfall. Show them the basics on how rain is measured. This video is for kids for basic details on a complicated process> https://www.youtube.com/watch?v=GgLatKFXyXQ

Brilliant Screen-Free Stuff to do With Kids

RIDDLES – BRAIN BUSTER RIDDLES FOR VERY SMART KIDS

The answers are in the last chapter of this book

Joey's Dad and Mom have 4 children. The first child's name is Sunday, the second child's name is Monday, and the third child's name is Tuesday. What is the name of their fourth child?

(*Again, all answers are in the last chapter of this book*)

*

On a table, three playing cards are lying next to each other. There is a 2 to the right of a king. There is a diamond to the left of a spade. There is an ace to the left of a heart and there is a heart to the left of a spade.

What are the three cards? (Use a pencil and paper and draw a diagram to help you figure this out).

*

A sundial has no moving parts and is a way to tell the time. What timepiece has the most moving parts of any timepiece?

*

What is round and flat and has two eyes but cannot see?

*

What type of cheese is made backward?

*

When I'm first spoken, I am a mystery. When the mystery is solved, no one is serious. What am I?

*

When you look in my face, you will not see anything else except me looking at you and I can't lie.

*

Joey stood next to a tree and marked his height by writing his name on the bark three years ago. This tree grows at the rate of 6 inches per year and now four years later, Joey stands 3 inches taller than the mark where he wrote his name on the bark three years ago.

How much has Joey grown in three years?

*

A local candy store sells the most delicious red candy hearts ever made and lets children exchange 3 red candy heart wrappers for one brand-new red candy heart. Joey wants to earn red candy hearts and decides to collect red candy heart wrappers from other kids so he can get free red candy hearts.

What is the least number of wrappers for Joey to collect to get and eat 10 red candy hearts?

*

This next one seems difficult but it is really easy!

There is a lake which is covered with lily pads which grew in the lake over time. Every day, the lily pad growth would double in size.

If it took 100 days for the lily pads to cover all of the lake, how long does it take for the lily pads to cover one-half the lake?

*

You are sitting still in a car. All the windows are closed and there are no vents that would allow a breeze or wind to enter the inside of the car. You have tied a helium balloon with a string to the floor of the car. You start the engine and accelerate. Will the helium balloon move back, forward or stay in the same place?

*

You have a glass of water that has one ice cube in it and the ice cube is floating and gradually melting. When the ice cube melts completely will the water rise, decrease, or stay the same?

*

Can you think of a word you can read forward, backward and upside down and still be read as the same word?

*

Here is an easy one. You wake up in the morning and are getting dressed. You need a pair of socks and in your drawer, there are 10 blue socks and 10 brown socks. You are unable to look in the drawer and can only pick one sock at a time. How many times do you have to pick a sock before you have a pair of the same color?

*

You are on your way to visit your Aunt on her birthday and she lives at the end of the valley. You have made several cakes for her and you want to bring the cakes to her for her birthday.

Between your house and her house, there are 5 bridges and there is a troll under each of the 5 bridges. Each troll will ask you to pay a toll before you can cross the bridge. The toll to cross the bridge is one cake. The trolls are nice and after you cross the bridge, they will give you back half of the cakes you were carrying before you paid them a toll.

Do you know how many cakes you need to carry at the start of your trip so you will have 2 cakes when you reach your Aunt's house?

*

Your Dad and Mom have 6 sons (including yourself). Each son has one sister. What is the total number of people in your family?

*

Mr. Brown was killed on Sunday afternoon. The people around him were asked what they were doing at the time he was killed.

His wife said she was reading, the butler said he was taking a shower, the chef said he was making breakfast, the maid said she was folding clothes, and the gardener said he was planting tomatoes. Which one is lying?

*

On the lighter side, **"If it's zero degrees outside today and it's supposed to be twice as cold tomorrow, how cold is it going to be?"** — Comedian Steven Wright

SAFETY SLOGANS TO SHARE

Teach the importance of safety. Here are well-known safety slogans you probably have heard but they are important, of course. Say these slogans out loud and ask the kids to repeat the slogan out loud back to you.

"The safe way is the best way."

"If you think safety rules are a pain, try having an accident."

"It's better to correct an unsafe friend than to visit them in the hospital. Be safe."

"Always play safely since you might not get a second chance."

"Get Smart, Use Safety from the Start."

"No safety? Know pain!

"The 'Safe Way' is the 'Best Way.'"

"When in doubt, check it out!"

And the well-known, "It's Better to be Safe than Sorry!"

Ask the kids what their favorite slogan is and why.

Teach safe procedures. It's worthwhile to teach your kids and grandkids these short emergency procedures that follow.

Dial 911. Make sure they know how to dial 911 (or other emergency phone numbers in your country) so they know how to get help if someone is seriously injured, passes out, or anything serious happens.

Strangers. Teach them not to answer the door to a stranger and to always get an adult to answer the door and not to open the door to any stranger.

Fires – Home fire drills. Stay away from matches, lighters, a hot iron, and let an adult know if any of these are lying around. Teach them to stay low to the floor and the safe ways to exit and practice them. Teach them about smoke alarms.

Stop Drop and Roll. In case their clothes catch fire, show them how to "Stop, Drop & Roll.">https://en.wikipedia.org/wiki/Stop,_drop_and_roll

Electrical Outlets. Teach them not to poke them with anything especially metal objects or try to plug something in with wet hands. Show them how plastic safety caps or covers are used to cover outlets.

Hot stovetops. Teach them the dangers of hot burners, hot pans, hot ovens, etc.

Microwaves. Talk about these and avoid putting any in a microwave.

- Paper bags can catch fire.
- Takeout containers with metal handles, aluminum foil (or anything metal) will spark, cause a fire and damage.
- Very thin plastic containers, or Styrofoam can melt and release chemicals into the food.

- Raw eggs in their shells, grapes, or anything uncovered in a bowl might explode.
- Chile peppers when heated release harmful chemicals which irritate your eyes.
- If the microwave is empty and turned on with nothing in it, this may damage the microwave or even cause a fire.

Safety slogan quiz. Give the kids or grandkids a quiz on safety slogans. Ask them the first part of the slogan and see if they remember and tell you the second part,

Q. The safe way is…?

A. The best way.

Q. If you think safety rules are a pain…?

A. Try having an accident.

Q. It's better to correct an unsafe friend than to...?

A. Visit them in the hospital. Be safe.

Q. Always play safely since you might not what...?

A. Get a second chance.

Q. Get Smart, Use Safety when...?

A. From the Start.

Q. No safety...?

A. Know pain!

Q. The 'Safe Way' is what...?

A. The Best Way.

Q. When in doubt...?

A. Check it out!

Q. It's Better to be Safe than what...?

A. Than be sorry!

Crime prevention and safety tips. This site has crime prevention tips and information on the basic safety rules every child should know.>https://www.safety.com/crime-prevention-tips-for-kids/

Playground safety. There's practical information on playground safety on this site in an article written by Kate M. Cronan, M.D., an Emergency Room Physician, explaining rules to keep children safe on playgrounds >https://kidshealth.org/en/parents/playground.html

SCIENCE FUN

Children love new things and the magic of science experiments is amazing to them.

ADULT SUPERVISION IS NEEDED FOR THESE EXPERIMENTS.

Making Magic Crystals. Pour one cup of Epsom salt into a bowl and one cup of hot water from your tap (Not boiling water, just the hottest water you can get from the tap). Continually stir the mixture for at least 1 ½ to 2 minutes. Continue stirring until <u>most</u> of the Epsom salt granules are dissolved.

Then pour the mixture into separate glasses (you can try this with one glass or several) and add food coloring to each glass using a different color of food coloring in each glass. Then place each glass in the freezer for 15 minutes. After 15 minutes, move the glasses to the refrigerator to stay there overnight. In the morning you will have beautifully colored crystals.

You will notice the crystals have grown overnight. Here is the science behind it.

Epsom salts are magnesium sulfate granules that dissolve in the water and the hotter the water is from the tap; the more salts will be dissolved. When the mixture is cooled rapidly, the atoms in the magnesium sulfate collide with each other causing a crystal structure.

Ivory soap - make a puffy cloud soap bar. Take a bar of Ivory Soap and cut it into several pieces (4-5 approximately equal pieces). Place the pieces equidistant apart on a plate and put it in the microwave for about 2 minutes on high. Watch the Ivory soap expand in the microwave. Stop the microwave once the soap has stopped expanding (otherwise it will start to burn).

The soap will expand into a puffy cloud because of the small air molecules inside Ivory soap. Allow it to cool. The soap can still be used normally in its puffy cloud shape. Ivory soap has little air pockets in it along with a small amount of moisture in each pocket. As the microwave heats it, the water vaporizes and the air in the small pockets expands causing the Ivory Soap bar to take a cloud-like shape.

Carnations coloring themselves. Start with 4 white carnations (more if you like) and four 16 oz plastic cups of water. Fill each cup halfway. Add 3 drops of food coloring (use different colors) in each cup. Clean cut the stem of each carnation and place one carnation in each cup. Come back in an hour and observe the carnations. Leave them overnight and observe them in the morning. The petals will be gradually taking on the color of the food coloring.

Try adding more food coloring (say 6 drops to each cup) and see what happens.

Leave the carnation for another day or so to see how long it takes to have the carnation completely color itself to match the food coloring.

Each carnation has its own "elevator" that is called the Xylem that transports water up the stem to the leaves of the flower.

You can also slit the stem into 2 or more stems and place each slit stem into a separate colored glass of food coloring. This will result in 2 or more colors being combined in the petals as different colored water is drawn into the flower from each piece of stem.

Fizzy Oranges. Cut an orange into wedges and put them on a plate. Put a small dish of baking soda next to them. Dip an orange slice into the baking soda and bite the orange slice. This will create an orange fizz in your mouth. This is because oranges have citric acid and baking soda is a base. When they are mixed, millions of tiny bubbles of carbon dioxide are released giving the inside of your mouth a fizzing sensation.

Rainstorm in a glass. Fill a glass halfway with clear water and put shaving cream in an even layer over the water that is in the glass. Fill enough shaving cream to reach the top of the glass. Smooth off any excess shaving cream with a plastic knife or spoon.

In a separate cup, mix a half cup of water with 9 drops of food coloring. Take a small spoon and gently spread the colored water from the cup over the top of the shaving cream and see what happens.

As you gradually add small spoons of colored water on the top of the shaving cream the colored water gets too heavy for the shaving cream to hold the colored water on top of it, and a rainstorm is created in the glass.

In other words, as you gradually and gently added water to the top of the shaving cream, that water becomes too heavy for the shaving cream and you create your own rainstorm!

The clouds in our skies are loaded with water. But, like shaving cream, they cannot hold very, very heavy amounts of water and clouds rain when the water is too heavy.

More Easy Science Experiments for Kids. There are many easy and fascinating science experiments for kids online like this YouTube with 18 amazing experiments you can do at home>https://www.youtube.com/watch?v=BjHqeh4ZuyA

SNOW – FUN IN THE SNOW

Sledding & Tobogganing. Good simple family fun for everyone! Most adults remember the childhood thrills of speeding downhill on a sled or steep toboggan runs. Bring hot chocolate in a thermos too!

Snow Sculptures. On fresh fallen or clean snow, get separate spray bottles of water with different colors of food coloring in each. Choose as many colors as you wish. Create sculptures, drawings and artworks in the snow by spraying the snow with different colors.

This site has ice sculptures, snow sculptures, and interesting snow creations to expand your thoughts on what the kids can create in the snow.> https://www.backyardboss.net/best-snow-sculpture-ideas/

Use your imagination on your creations and see what happens. Take pictures.

Big Snowball Roll. Have a contest to see who can create the largest snowball. The children start with approximately the same sized snowball and then enlarge it by rolling it through the snow. After the children create several large snowballs, you can use the large snowballs in the next section for making snow people!

Creating snow people. Instead of making the usual snowman, ask the kids to create replicas of themselves, you, or the entire family. Roll appropriately sized snowballs or use the ones created from the previous section. Color the snow people with food coloring in spray bottles and decorate it! They can give the snow people rosy cheeks, brown curly hair, etc.

Suggest they also create replicas of anyone they wish to such as their classmates, teachers, ministers, etc. Ask them to create snow animals too!

Creating snow people and animals is fun and don't forget the hats, scarfs, button noses, etc!

For more laughs, you can decorate the snow people as if they were lying down in the snow, or even standing on their head. For an upside-down snowperson, remember to put the eyes, nose, etc. inverted and add stick arm branches and fingers in the ground to support holding the snowperson standing on its head!

Snowpeople fashion show. Make a runway in the snow and dress snow people in high fashions!

Pin the nose on the snowman. Like pin the tail on the donkey. Blindfold one of the children and ask the blindfolded child to pin the nose on the snowman. This game can go longer if you ask them to pin the eyes, ears, mouth, scarf, hat, etc. on the snowman too! Take pictures!

Snowball toss. Instead of the usually snowball fight (that's fun of course too!), draw a line in the snow or mark it with a stick. Then in front of the line, make 6 circles in the snow with each circle being further away from the line. Have the children stand behind the line and take turns tossing a snowball into each circle. See who's the first to toss a snowball into each circle.

Instead of drawing circles in the snow, you can use buckets instead. Or if you have food coloring in spray bottles, paint a bullseye target and assign points from the outside ring inward to the bullseye.

Snowball target practice. Put cans or other objects on a fence and step back and see who can toss a snowball and knock off all the objects on the fence.

Tic Tac Toe in the snow. A very simple game that adds to the varieties of things to do when it snows. Draw a Tic Tac Toe diagram in the snow for each game.

Shovel snow for the unfortunate. Teach the children charitable acts and good deeds by suggesting they shovel snow off the sidewalks, driveway, stairs of neighbors who can't shovel around their own home.

Start a snow shoveling business. For older kids, suggest they begin a snow shoveling business. Ask them first to do a simple business plan to plan out what they will charge (by the hour or by a set fee depending on the area to be shoveled) as most people prefer a negotiated set fee. Have them plan out how they will market their services – will they go door to door with personal solicitation with snow shovels in hand? Will they do telemarketing, signs, leaflets, etc. Who will be their target customers?

Generally, teach the children about business, accounting, financing (do they need a loan for more shovels, equipment, etc.) advertising costs, marketing, franchising, competition, etc.

Ask them to estimate revenue, expenses and their anticipated profit. This site has a lot of ideas and guidance for kids about business http://bizkids.com/

Make hot chocolate with snow. Instead of using water, give them containers and ask them to fill the container up with fresh fallen clean snow and bring it inside where you melt the snow in a saucepan and bring it to a boil for three minutes or more. The little ones like to watch the snow rapidly melt in a pan. Then add a hot chocolate mix.

Snowball fights and snow fortresses. Snowball fights are a lot of fun! Have them build a snow fortress to hide behind with a large front fortress wall. See who can build the most elaborate fortress (with secret observation holes, high defense battlements, secret escape passages, ample snowball storage, etc.).

They will learn about architecture and design. Check out this site on snow forts > https://www.wikihow.com/Build-a-Snow-Fort

Snow amusement parks. Kids love amusement parks, carnivals, winter parks, etc. Ask them to create in the snow by building their own miniature amusement park with ski jumps, ice skating rinks, toboggan slides, cafes, etc. Ask them to create it all in miniature size for whatever they imagine.

Snow towns. Ask them to build their own miniature "Snowville" or "Terry's Town" and teach them about land planning and ask them to construct a miniature snow town.

Tell them about residential areas, commercial areas, town halls, schools, courthouses, police stations, fire stations, water treatment plants, etc. This site has development information about responsible land use and land planning

> https://study.com/academy/lesson/uses-of-land-lesson-for-kids.html

Identify and photograph animal tracks in the snow. If you're in the woods or a park, ask them to search for animal tracks in the snow and see if they can take pictures of ones they don't know much about. There are many sites online about the tracks of animals> https://www.greenbelly.co/pages/animal-tracks-identification-guide

Follow the very cool (but silly) leader. A funny and silly game! Have them line up with one adult in front and one adult in the back of the line and go through the snow asking them to follow and imitate your very cool moves. Be creative and start with things like a high-knee march, followed by waddling like a duck, then crawl on all fours, etc. Take turns being the leader. LOL!

Tug of War in the Snow. Probably safer than a tug of war on grass or pavement and a lot of fun!

Build a snow picnic table. Build a snow picnic table with snow chairs, snow benches, etc. Make snow plates, utensils, bowls, and even snow sandwiches!

Snow soccer. Played the same as regular soccer by kicking a ball through the goal in the snowfield.

Snow Dodgeball. Played the same as regular dodgeball. If you don't have a dodgeball to toss back and forth, use a snowball instead.

Snowball toss and pyramid cup tower. Build a tower of paper cups on the snow with 5 cups at the base (worth 5 points each), 4 cups on top of the 5 bottom cups (worth 4 points each), 3 cups on top of the 4 (worth 3 points each), 2 cups on top of the 3 (worth 1 point each), and 1 cup on the 2 (worth 1 point). Draw the point value on each cup.

Stand an appropriate distance from the tower according to kids' ages. Stagger the lines they stand behind with younger kids closer. Toss snowballs to knock down cups and keep score in the snow. Do a coin toss to determine the throwing order. Do it with teams too.

STORYTELLING FUN

Storytelling will help solve present or future problems and help kids better understand the world. Storytelling also develops their verbal skills, builds their confidence, and improves their public speaking ability.

Begin by you telling a story about how you met your husband or wife. Were you very nervous? How did you handle it? Were you swept off your feet? Kids enjoy learning family history and a great story will make your relationship grow stronger. It helps the grandkids develop a strong family history.

Tell a story about when you were a child. A personal story especially from grandparents about how you dealt with things when you were the child's age is more fun than reading a book every night before going to sleep and your story will be remembered.

For example, tell a story about your first day at school, or when you learned to swim, or caught your first fish, etc. You will become closer even though you may not realize it at first.

Tell a story about when the child was born. Moms can tell a great story about this and dads too. For grandparents, tell a story where you were when you first heard your grandchild was born? Where were you? What did you do? When did you first see your grandchild and what did he or she look like when you first saw them? What did your grandchild do when you first held them?

Grandparents can tell a story about their early experiences with their grandchild. Were you there when they first learned to walk and talk? What did they say for their first words to you? Kids love to hear stories about themselves.

Grandparents, tell them a story your grandparents or parents told you. These stories should fascinate them. Give details as far as you remember on how you were told the stories. Explain to them what things were like back then.

Tell them what your parents and grandparents were like. Were they immigrants? How old were they when they settled here? And, tell your grandkids to pass these stories on to their children and grandchildren.

Tell a story about your first day at your first job. How did you get the job? What was your interview like? How did you dress? How much were you paid? What was your second job and how did you eventually get into your lifetime job? How did you feel about it?

Tell a story about how you solved an issue. Did you have trouble with math? Were kids making fun of you at school? Were you ever bullied at school? Tell them how you dealt with it. Your story may get them to voluntarily tell you about issues they are going through which you didn't know about. Your story will be remembered well.

Tell a story about how you solved a nagging problem. Were you a smoker? Were you overweight? Did the other kids like you or not like you? Why? How did you deal with each situation?

Tell a story about what you liked as a kid. What did you like to do the most when you were your grandchild's age? What funny childhood events happened to you? Who was your first friend and how did you become friends?

Ask your children or grandchildren to tell you a story. If they enjoy your stories, ask them to tell you a story about school, or sports, or whatever you think appropriate.

Tell a story on how you got in trouble at school. How embarrassed were you? What did the others say? How did you solve it? Why won't you ever do it again?

Tell a story that made you proud. Building self-confidence is important for kids. What made you confident? What was the first award or win you ever had? How did you handle it? Tell them about old sayings, "When you lose, talk very little. When you win, talk less." Tell them about sportsmanship and how winning and losing may not be important as the old saying goes, "The good thing about losing is that it's only temporary, and the bad thing about winning is that it's only temporary."

SWIMMING POOL FUN

Create Your Own Synchronized Swimming, Swim Dance or Water Ballet. Girls love this! Ask the girls to create and choreograph their own synchronized swimming or water ballet. Or just a simple pool dance they create themselves. They need to think up and agree on a name for their routine as well like, "The Very Cool Little Mermaid Water Ballet" etc.

Ask them to pick out a song and see if they can choreograph their performance. Take a video. It's something they will remember all their lives.

Solo Swimmer – Things to Do. If you are the ever-present lifeguard and the child is the only one in the pool and bored, give the child a list of things to accomplish and tell the child they will get a small reward after finishing the list. The list should show things like swim 10 laps, dive for and recover 5 objects in the deep end of the pool, swim the width (or length) of the pool underwater, sit on the bottom of the pool for the count of 5 (or more), practice doing under the water somersaults, do a handstand, make a big splash (cannonball!), jump out into the water and twist 180 degrees in the air before hitting the water, etc.

Play music. Whether your child or grandchild is the sole swimmer or swimming with others, background music helps to keep everyone upbeat and in a great mood.

Underwater camera. If you happen to have an underwater waterproof camera, suggest the children swimming alone or children swimming together to take pictures of objects in the water, sinking in the water, or at the bottom of the pool, videos of objects sinking, etc. Photos/videos of someone jumping in the pool taken underwater are a lot of fun if your camera is waterproof. Play the video in slow motion, fast motion, and in reverse too!

Beach ball or water polo ball race. Have them race pushing a beach ball or a water polo ball from one side of the pool to the other (and back again too if you wish). Or, exercise doing laps with a water polo ball up and down the pool. This will use up a lot of their awesome youthful energy!

Ping Pong ball pool race. Kids line up at one end of the pool with each having a ping pong ball. They jump in the pool and race to the other end blowing the ping pong ball to the other side of the pool. The one whose ping pong ball reaches the other side first wins.

Keep fit with Pool Volleyball. It's lots of fun and helps keep everyone fit.

Towel on head tag game. This is played like a game of tag only those playing must all fold up a towel and balance it on their heads. One person is designated as the chaser who chases and tags another player and whoever he tags becomes the new chaser. If a chaser loses his towel, he remains the chaser until he tags another player with the towel still on his head. If another player loses the towel off his head trying to avoid the chaser, the first child to lose his towel becomes the new chaser.

TEACH SOMETHING MEMORABLE

Teach them a skill. Try different things to see what they like and when they are keen on something, teach them more about it whether it be knitting, loving to read, cooking, baking, woodworking, photography, stamp collecting, sports, how to fix a car or change the oil, using tools, drills, wrenches, how to work crossword puzzles, or, whatever they enjoy and take an interest in. You might be initiating a lifelong hobby or occupation for them.

Ride a bike. If they haven't learned how to ride a bike yet, teach them. They will remember their whole life who taught them. Learning to ride is, of course, a super thrilling experience for them!

Teach them to swim. Many local pools have "Learn to swim" classes which are very effective. If your grandchild hasn't learned to swim yet take him to a local swimming pool. Here is a site with very detailed step by step instructions on teaching a child to swim > https://www.wikihow.com/Teach-Your-Child-to-Swim

And teach them how to use a mask and snorkel too to open up the underwater world for them!

Teach them to cook. Start simple and teach them as your mother or grandmother taught you. Here is a site with suggestions on dishes to prepare themselves appropriate for their ages> https://www.eatright.org/homefoodsafety/four-steps/cook/teaching-kids-to-cook

Ancestry. Draw a family tree for them. Tell them what you know about your ancestors and others in your family. Kids usually love these stories especially if you tell them lots of details on how things were many years ago.

"Every day of our lives we make deposits into the minds and thoughts of our children." – Charles Swindoll

TEEN ACTIVITIES

Teens spend a lot of time with other teens sharing experiences as they transition to adulthood.

Teens can feel isolated and be drawn to grandparents to seek an elder's advice. Consequently, grandparents spending time one on one such as a nature walk and discussing life in general is very valuable to teens as well as giving grandparents (who may also feel isolated) time together to support each other.

Aviation and Aerobatic Flying. Teens usually have a strong interest in Aviation and see the first chapter of this book for activities to share and form a close bond with your teen or teen grandchild. Introduce them to the world of private aviation.

Check with local aerobatic flight schools to learn if you can view their maneuvers and perhaps go up for an initial ride. The International Aerobatic Club is the largest aerobatic club in the world and most likely has information on aerobatic clubs near you. https://www.iac.org/aerobatic-flight-schools

Bridging the gap with questions. Teens tend to keep to themselves when there is a large age gap. If you want the teen to be more open, here are some sample and random questions that may get the teen talking more and discussing his or her life with you. NOTE: We use the masculine gender in pronouns for convenience in these questions, but these questions apply to both genders.

- After generally asking how things are going, ask what he sees himself doing 5 or 10 years from now.
- What does he like to do most? Why? Does it make him happy? What other things make him happy?
- What makes him angry or most annoyed in situations?
- What do you think about bullies?
- Do you believe in true love?
- What makes you really laugh hard?

- Do you think you'll get married and have kids one day?
- Do you procrastinate? If so, what if anything motivates you the most.
- How do you handle stressful situations? Can you keep cool in difficult situations?
- How are your teachers treating you at school? Which teacher do you like the most? Why? Which teacher do you dislike the most? Why?
- Who is your best friend? Why are you best friends?
- Have you set any goals for yourself this year?
- Do you see others cheating at school? How do you handle that?
- Do you think being fit and exercising is important to you?
- Is there any subject you would like to learn more about at school?

- Is there any subject you would like to learn less about at school?
- What person do you most admire and want to be like?
- If you could meet anyone whether alive or dead, who would you like to meet and talk to and what would you talk about?

Show your teen grandchild a photo of yourself as a teen. If you have a photo of yourself as a teen, bring it along and show it to your grandchild. Your teen photo will most likely open the door for you and your teen to tell stories on a one to one basis. If you had certain favorite dance moves, show your dance moves and ask the grandchild to show you theirs.

Be positive. Try to avoid criticism. Criticizing a teen can lead to low self-esteem which may even make a teen rebel more or put up his defensives. Positive reinforcement is better and be sure to remember to applaud good behavior and do what you can to increase their self-esteem.

Grandparents, tell stories on how you transitioned to an adult. If the conversation turns to you, and you have an opportunity to discuss your life you might want to tell stories about yourself. How did you get through high school and university? What were your difficult subjects? Was your social life difficult? Were you popular or unpopular? How did you meet grandma? What was your career like? What was raising kids like?

Go to a sporting event together. Pick an event that strongly interests your grandchild and get two tickets (e.g. sports, theatre, etc.). Afterward, go to a restaurant and talk about the event and ask your grandchild their opinion on the event. What was the most exciting part? What went wrong mostly if your team or side lost? Show the teen you value their opinion very highly helping to increase their confidence level.

Fishing, Hiking, Gardening, Cooking, Exploring trips. Choose a trip or an activity where you both get away from everyone doing something your grandchild likes. Show respect for their ability, fitness, agility, multi-tasking, etc.

Minute to Win It Games. These games are very popular with teens (as well as most kids) and originated from an international game show franchise. The games involve 60-second challenges using objects commonly found around the home. The games are fun, simple, and can be done in a series of one-minute games so that when one challenge is completed the participants quickly race and go on to the next challenge. There are too many different Minute to Win It games to list in this book. This site (and many other sites) have a large assortment of Minute to Win It Games and they are lots of LOL fun > https://toodrie.com/minute-to-win-it-games-for-teens/

Ask for help with your computer. Most teens are great at computers and have them teach you something that's important to you. Consider giving them a reward or compensation if it is a time-consuming job for them.

Attend their events. If your grandchild is getting an award or helping at a sporting event or cheerleading or playing in the band, etc. your attendance to these events shows you care about your grandchild. Show them you are an avid fan of theirs.

Show unconditional love. Let them know you support them whether they get good grades or bad grades, succeed or fail, and tell them no one on earth ever wins or succeeds all the time. Tell them about your failures. Let them know you are on their side and they can count on you anytime.

Ask about their friends. The friends of your teen grandchild are extremely important, of course. Are they good people? Are they achievers? Are they on drugs, have bad habits, drink excessively, etc? Share stories about the bad friends you had as a teen. How did you deal with peer pressure? How did you get around refusing to engage or limit yourself taking drugs, tobacco, excessive alcohol, etc? Or if you engaged in bad habits how did you discontinue them?

Fine dining. If your grandchild hasn't had the experience or learned the protocol and social skills at fine dining restaurants, select one and give it a try. Order a bottle of wine too and teach them about food/wine pairing, etc. The experience will be valuable to them on dates, celebrating special events, prom evenings, etc.

Figure Skating, Bowling, Tennis, Soccer, etc. Most teens like sports as it builds teamwork and goal-setting skills, and exercise also releases stress. Playing sports builds confidence. Give them the opportunity and make it easy for them to participate in skating, bowling, swimming, etc. Grandparents may be able to better able to afford lessons for them too.

Parent/teen disputes. Usually it's best for grandparents to avoid taking sides and remain totally neutral if your grandchild tells you about a dispute they have with their parents. Listen and maintain respect for both views and show your unconditional love for parents and the teen.

Bonding with a teen grandchild – sharing mutual interests. If you know your granddaughter loves to create, you may want to share your special talents with her in more depth for crochet, pottery, knitting, graphic design, photography, or whatever they may be.

Ask your teen to interview you and store on StoryCorps.org. You can help prepare questions for your teen grandchild to ask you while the teen interviews you on an aspect of your life (especially a story on your teen years). Preserve your personal story on Storycorps.org > https://storycorps.org.

Cook together at a family event. A great opportunity to teach your signature dish to your grandchild and tell him or her to share it someday with their grandchildren! Or ask your grandchild to decide what to prepare for a family dinner get together and you and only you assist your grandchild. Give your grandchild lots of respect and admiration for their ingenuity and creativity.

Take a class together. Dabble.co offers a directory of classes both parents and grandparents. Your teen might have an interest in these classes whether it be woodworking, cooking, motorcycle workshop, yoga, meditation, etc. This is a great way to bond for life. > https://dabble.co/

Sharing Grandma's Jewelry with Teens. Most teen granddaughters would love to be able to share in wearing your jewelry especially if you have a large collection of jewelry you accumulated over the years. Show them your jewelry and share stories about how and where you acquired it and the meaning of it.

Read the same book. If you find your teen or teen grandchild has an interest in a certain author or a certain book, consider both of you reading the book at the same time and discussing it. You might be starting your own family book club!

TODDLER AND THREE TO FIVE-YEAR-OLD ACTIVITIES

Toddler presents in a bathroom bowl. Wrap several of the toddler toys in old gift paper and leave them in the bathroom in a large container. Every time the toddler properly uses the toilet, tell them they can unwrap a present. This helps toilet training.

Toddler tub party. Put inflatable water wings on your toddler for safety and comfort in the tub. Add floating large and safe toys, bubble bath, small or large beach ball and music.

Toddler toy stack. Start with 10 ordinary paper cups or plastic cups and demonstrate how they stack. Make different piles of stacks. Add more or take away some to make it different. If you have different bright colored cups that's great.

Spider web a doorway with sticky tape. Stretch tape across a doorway in a crisscross intersecting or spider web fashion. Give your toddler small crumpled paper and if you spread the tape thoroughly the paper will stick to the web. Cotton balls work too.

Simon says. Toddlers, as they grow, can understand this game and enjoy it very much with commands like, "Simon says touch your nose", "Simon says touch your arm" "Kiss your elbow" (no one can kiss their elbow), etc.

Number treasure hunt. Use post-it notes and write the numbers 1 through 10 (or whatever you like) on brightly colored post-it notes. Place the post-it notes around the house and ask them to find them. See if they can put them in order once they are found. Or see if they can collect them in numerical order.

Water glass xylophone. Fill glasses with different levels of water and show the children how to make different sounds tapping glasses with different water levels. Use a wooden spoon and lightly tap the glasses. Vary the water levels to create different tones. See this video on setting up a scale and playing songs

> https://www.youtube.com/watch?v=sIO-JhMvu6M

Cardboard box fort. Help your toddler and/or 3 to 5-year-old child have fun with a cardboard box. Cut a door, windows, skylight, etc. in a large empty cardboard box in any way they want. Kids enjoy going inside it! Ask them to decorate the inside and outside of the box as they like.

Dress up. Play the age-old dress up game and let your toddler and other kids dress in your clothes, put on your shoes, hats, etc. as they wish. Take pictures and show them years later.

Make popsicles. Make different colored drinks (e.g. with Kool-Aid) in an ice cube tray then put the tray in the freezer. After about 20 minutes, take out the tray and put popsicle sticks into each cube and return it to the freezer and wait until frozen.

Sidewalk chalk activities. Ask them to draw a picture of themselves, Or, ask them to lie down and trace their outline and enhance it and vice-versa.

Chalk draw mom and dad. Ask them to draw mom and dad, grandma and grandpa, Uncle Louie, etc. They can draw their house, their friends, their pets, their toys, etc.

Draw a bullseye target for bean bag toss. Draw a bullseye on the sidewalk and color it. Ask them to take turns tossing a bean bag to the target and keep score. Or, see who can get a bullseye first. Assign points for each concentric circle in the target.

Alphabet square word hop. Draw 26 squares with a letter in each square. Ask them to hop from letter to letter to make the word you call out, like, "s-e-e" "r-u-n" "s-u-n" "h-o-p" etc.

Trace letters. Three to five-year-old kids love to draw. Learn the alphabet and the sounds the letters make by tracing the letters of the alphabet and asking them for a word that begins with that letter.

Jigsaw Puzzles. A simple easy jigsaw puzzle with large pieces so they don't try to put them in their mouths help develop a child's problem-solving skills which they need throughout their life. They also help kids learn pattern recognition, motor skills. They also help kids develop critical-thinking skills, i.e., the ability to link ideas together which is also a very important life skill.

Warmer and Colder. This is the old search game when you hide a fun object, your toddler's favorite toy, or a treat and they search for it while you are telling them if they are getting warmer (closer) or colder (further away) from what they are searching for.

Scavenger hunt. A simple search game for objects familiar to your toddler is a lot of fun and add "warmer and colder" to keep the toddler's interest.

Hide and Seek. Always a favorite.

Toddler Dance Party. Helps develop their motor skills and coordination. Try fast tunes, slow tunes, songs with a heavy beat, songs with a light beat, and even classical music too. Dance in fast motion, slow motion, pause the music, etc.

TONGUE TWISTERS

Toddlers verbalizing. Place a tissue in front of your mouth and show your toddler the letter "P" and show how to make the "P" sound. Place a tissue over the front of your mouth and they will laugh seeing the tissue move when you make the sound. Have them take a turn and do it with other hard consonant letters like B, F, T, etc.

Help the toddler talk. Use a play phone and pretend you are talking to dad or grandma and hand the phone over. Hand the phone back and forth, and so on. Socializing with other toddlers helps too when they hear the words or sounds of other toddlers.

Toddler sing-along. A simple sing-along helps them remember words and encourages them to sing. Sing a tune and have them continue it as best they can. Hopefully, they'll have a favorite tune to practice over and over.

Tongue Twisters for kids improve pronunciation and confidence when speaking. Say these one-line tongue twisters slow at first, then practice saying them faster and faster!

"The big bumbling bear burned his butt baking bread."

*

"The cook took a good look at the cookbook."

*

"She sees cheese"

*

"Four fine fresh fish for you"

*

"He threw three free throws"

*

"Twelve twins twirled twelve twigs."

*

"If Freaky Fred Found Fifty Feet of Fruit

And Fed Forty Feet to his Friend Frank

How many Feet of Fruit did Freaky Fred Find?"

*

"A pleasant peasant presently presents you with a pleasant peasant's present."

For older kids, and adults, see who can say these 3 very tough tongue twisters 10 times slowly. It is a lot harder than you realize.

First tough one, "The top cop saw a cop top."

The second one, "I slit a sheet. A sheet I slit, and on the slitted sheet I sit."

The third one, "The sixth sick sheik's sixth sheep's sick."

Here are fun ones,

Six slippery snails slid slowly toward the sea.

*

Green glass globes glow greenly.

*

Double bubble gum doubles the bubbles.

*

Two tiny tired turtles trod to Tennessee.

VEGETABLE GARDEN FUN

Introduce your child or grandchild to vegetable gardens by creating a healthy garden (which will also beautify your yard as well and save money).

Children enjoy planting seeds, or seedlings and watching them grow. Take pictures as the garden develops.

Research and share with them what you want to plant and plan out the way you will arrange the garden. Tell them you are going to teach them how to create the "Mom's or Grandma's Magical and Healthy Vegetable Garden" (or whatever you want to name it).

First, draw a map of your vegetable garden and designate areas for each plant. Draw in walkways between the vegetable beds for easy access. Winter is a perfect time to <u>plan</u> your vegetable garden and ask them to help you map it out so you will know how many plants you will need in the Spring and space them out appropriately. They will be eagerly looking forward to the Springtime planting.

If you planted a garden before in the same space, discuss with them crop rotation which is avoiding planting vegetables of the same family each year in the same location.

Here is a list of vegetables you may want to consider along with the group they belong to, so you avoid planting vegetables of the same family year after year in the same location.

1. Onion family: chive, leeks, onions, and shallots.

2. Potato family: eggplant, peppers, potatoes, and tomatoes.

3. Mustard family: broccoli, cabbage, cauliflower, kale, kohlrabi, mustard greens, radish, rutabaga, spinach, and turnip.

4. Cucumber family: cucumbers, melons, pumpkin, and squash.

5. Bean family: beans and peas.

For additional help, there are many sites (e.g. Better Homes and Gardens articles, etc.) on the web showing you how to create eye-pleasing and colorful vegetable gardens.

Gardening also teaches kids how to use gardening tools and helps develop their motor skills and helps keep their fitness level up. They also learn how to grow their own food.

Kids also learn about responsibility and the necessity of proper maintenance. Creating a wonderful vegetable garden also gives them increased self-esteem and confidence.

Toddlers enjoy just digging in the dirt and you can teach a Toddler to learn patience by showing them not to pick vegetables (green tomatoes, small unripe berries, etc.) before they mature and ripen. Working in a garden with others also improves their social skills and learning to share the work and socializing.

This site has a 15 easy step by step plan for creating a functional and healthy vegetable garden. > https://www.wikihow.com/Start-a-Vegetable-Garden

Above all have fun with all your activities with kids. You're enriching their lives and your life too!

ANSWERS TO BRAIN BUSTER RIDDLES

Joey's Dad and Mom have 4 children. The first child's name if Sunday, the second child's name is Tuesday, and the third child's name is Tuesday. What is the name of their fourth child?

A. Joey. Since they have 4 children!

*

On a table, there are three playing cards lying next to each other. There is a 2 to the right of a king. There is a diamond to the left of a spade. There is an ace to the left of a heart and there is a heart to the left of a spade.

What are the three cards? (Use a pencil and paper and draw a diagram to help you figure this out if you can).

A. The cards are from left to right: An Ace of Diamonds, a King of Hearts, and a Two of Spades.

*

A sundial has no moving parts and is a way to tell the time. What have the most moving parts of any timepiece?

A. An hourglass since it has more moving grains of sand than you can count.

What is round and flat and has two eyes but cannot see?

A. A button.

*

What type of cheese is made backward?

A. Edam (spell it backward).

*

When I'm first spoken, I am a mystery. When the mystery is solved, no one is serious. What am I?

A. A riddle.

*

When you look in my face, you will not see anything else except me looking at you and I can't lie.

A. A reflection of yourself.

*

Joey stood next to a tree and marked his height by writing his name on the bark three years ago. This tree grows at the rate of 6 inches per year and now four years later, Joey stands 3 inches taller than the mark where he wrote his name on the bark three years ago.

How much has Joey grown in three years?

A. Trees grow from their tops. The place where Joey wrote his name to mark his height has not moved in three years. Therefore, Joey has grown 3 inches more.

*

A local candy store that sells the most delicious red candy hearts ever made and lets children exchange 3 red candy heart wrappers for one brand-new red candy heart. Joey wants to earn red candy hearts and decides to collect red candy heart wrappers from other kids so he can get free red candy hearts.

What is the least number of wrappers for Joey to collect in order to get and eat 10 red candy hearts?

A. If you get one red candy heart for 3 candy wrappers Joey would need 10 x 3 = 30 wrappers to get 10 red candy hearts. But Joey only needs 21 wrappers at the beginning and not 30. This is because he can use 21 wrappers to get 7 red candy hearts and after he eats the 7, he will have 7 more empty wrappers. He can then use the 7 empty wrappers to get 2 more red candy hearts and have one wrapper left over. After he eats the 2 more red candy hearts, he will have two more empty wrappers and those plus the extra wrappers will make 3 empty wrappers. He then uses these 3 wrappers to get one more red candy heart and that makes a total of 10!

*

There is a lake which is covered with lily pads. The lily pads grow on the lake over time. Every day, the lily pads would double in size.

If it took 100 days for the lily pads to cover all of the lake, how long does it take for the lily pads to cover one-half the lake?

A. 99 days. Since the lily pads doubled in size every day, on the 99th day the lily pads must have been over half the size of the lake, and then doubled so on the 100th day the entire lake was covered.

*

You are sitting still in a car. All the windows are closed and there are no vents that would allow a breeze or wind to enter the inside of the car. You have tied a helium balloon with a string to the floor of the car. You start the engine and accelerate. Will the helium balloon move back, forward or stay in the same place?

A. Believe it or not, the balloon will move forward. The helium balloon floats in the air because the helium in the balloon is less dense than air and gravity pulls the denser air to the ground making the helium balloon float in the air. When the car is accelerated, gravity pulls the denser air backward toward the back of the car which makes the helium balloon move forward when the car is accelerated forward.

If the car slightly accelerated backward the helium balloon would move slightly backward too since the denser air would be moving forward in the car.

*

You have a glass of water that has one ice cube in it and the ice cube is floating and gradually melting. When the ice cube melts completely will the water rise, decrease, or stay the same?

A. The water level will remain the same. This is because the exact amount of water that the ice cube displaces is equal to its mass and the extra water from the melting ice cube will be the same as the amount of water the ice cube displaced.

*

Can you think of a word you can read forward, backward and upside down and still be read as the same word?

A. NOON

*

You wake up in the morning and are getting dressed. You need a pair of socks and in your drawer, there are 10 blue socks and 10 brown socks. You are unable to look in the drawer and can only pick one sock at a time. How many times do you have to pick a sock before you have a pair of the same color?

A. Three times. After you pick twice, you will have two socks and if they match you will have a pair. If they do not match, when you pick the third time you will have a sock that matches one of the socks you have already picked.

*

You are on your way to visit your Aunt on her birthday and she lives at the end of the valley. You have made several cakes for her and you want to bring the cakes to her for her birthday.

Between your house and her house, there are 5 bridges and there is a troll under each of the 5 bridges. Each troll will ask you to pay a toll before you can cross the bridge. The toll to cross the bridge is one cake. But the trolls are nice and after you cross the bridge, they will give you back half of the cakes you were carrying before you paid them a toll.

Do you know how many cakes you need to carry at the start of your trip so you will have 2 cakes when you reach your Aunt's house?

A. You leave with 2 cakes. Before crossing a bridge, you give one of the cakes to the troll. After you cross the bridge the troll will give you back half of the number of cakes you were carrying before you paid the toll and since you were carrying 2 cakes when you paid the toll, the troll will give you back one cake. Then as you approach the next bridge you will again be carrying 2 cakes, and you give one to the troll and at the end of the bridge, you will get back one cake from the troll, and so on. Eventually, you will arrive at your Aunt's house with exactly 2 cakes.

*

Your Dad and Mom have 6 sons (including yourself. Each son has one sister. What is the total number of people in your family?

A. The answer is a total of 9 persons. Mom and Dad, 6 sons and one daughter are a total of 9 people. All the sons have one sister (not 6 sisters).

*

Mr. Brown was killed on Sunday afternoon. The people around him were asked what they were doing at the time he was killed.

His wife said she was reading, the butler said he was taking a shower, the chef said he was making breakfast, the maid said she was folding clothes, and the gardener said he was planting tomatoes. Which one is lying?

A. The chef. The questions said the murder happened in the afternoon and the chef claimed he was making breakfast.

About the Authors

We hope you enjoyed this activity idea book and use it often for ways to get kids off-screen and balance their play activities.

Team Golfwell and Bruce Miller, B.A., J.D. are bestselling authors and have published over 35 books on various subjects. Their books have won awards and they have had several #1 bestsellers in Golf Coaching, Children's Sports Coaching, Sports Humor, and other categories. They live in New Zealand.

Contact us at Bruce@TeamGolfwell.com for anything. We love to hear from our fans!

Thank you very much for your interest in our book and we hope you enjoyed it.

If you liked our book and have the time, we would appreciate your leaving a brief review on Amazon, Goodreads or Barnes & Noble.

Have fun!

Thank you again very much!

[1] "American Academy of Pediatrics Announces New Recommendations for Children's Media Use", 2016. https://www.aap.org/en-us/about-the-aap/aap-press-room/Pages/American-Academy-of-Pediatrics-Announces-New-Recommendations-for-Childrens-Media-Use.aspx

[2] Science Daily, "Importance of good sleep routines for children," https://www.sciencedaily.com/releases/2018/12/181203080327.htm

[3] Ibid.

[4] Lydia Denworth and Brian Waves, PsychologyToday, https://www.psychologytoday.com/us/blog/brain-waves/201801/the-connection-between-writing-and-sleep

[5] Supra. https://www.sciencedaily.com/releases/2018/12/181203080327.htm

[6] Mayo Clinic, Healthy Lifestyle, Children's Health, https://www.mayoclinic.org/healthy-lifestyle/childrens-health/in-depth/child-sleep/art-20044338

[7] NCBI, National Institute on Health, "Youth screen media habits and sleep: sleep-friendly screen-behavior recommendations for clinicians, educators, and parents", April 1, 2019, April 1, 2019, https://www.ncbi.nlm.nih.gov/pmc/articles/PMC5839336/

[8] Harvard Health Publishing, Harvard Medical School, https://www.health.harvard.edu/mind-and-mood/more-evidence-that-exercise-can-boost-mood

[9] "Journaling for Mental Health," University of Rochester Medical School, https://www.urmc.rochester.edu/encyclopedia/content.aspx?ContentID=4552&ContentTypeID=1

[10] NASA, "Global Climate Change," https://climate.nasa.gov/evidence/

[11] National Autism Awareness Month: Incorporating Exercise, https://ymcaharrisburg.org/national-autism-awareness-month-incorporating-exercise/

[12] Supra.

[13] Inc. Article on "Read to young children in this way, and they'll develop greater intellectual empathy -- and become more successful," https://www.inc.com/bill-murphy-jr/neuroscience-kids-success-parents-best-practices.html

[14] Science Daily, A 'million-word gap for children who aren't read to at home, April 4, 2019 https://www.sciencedaily.com/releases/2019/04/190404074947.htm

[15] BBC, Science and Environment, "All you need to know about nature deficit disorder", https://www.bbc.com/news/science-environment-38094186

www.ingramcontent.com/pod-product-compliance
Lightning Source LLC
Chambersburg PA
CBHW071351290426
44108CB00014B/1503